CAPTAIN
AT KIAWAH

CAPTAIN AT KIAWAH

Bernard Gallacher
with Renton Laidlaw

Foreword by Sean Connery

CHAPMANS

Chapmans Publishers Ltd
141-143 Drury Lane
London WC2B 5TB

First published by Chapmans in 1991
Copyright © Bernard Gallacher with Renton Laidlaw 1991

A CIP Catalogue record for this book is
available from the British Library

ISBN 1-85592-566-4

Editor Tim Jollands
Design by ACE Limited
Course diagrams by Ken Lewis
Production by Geoff Barlow
Keyboarding by Wilcom Services
Typset in Janson Text by Dorchester Typesetting
Printed and bound in Great Britain
by Butler & Tanner Ltd, Frome, Somerset

PHOTOGRAPHIC ACKNOWLEDGEMENTS
Thanks are due to the following for allowing their copyright material to be reproduced in
the book: Allsport/David Cannon 101b, 102a, 103d, Allsport/Simon Bruty 103c, 103e;
Yours in Sport/Lawrence Levy 97, 98a, 98c, 98d, 99a, 99c, 99e, 102b, 102c, 102d, 103b,
Yours in Sport/Michael Cohen 99b, 104, Yours in Sport/Danielle Fleur 100c, 101a, 103a;
Phil Sheldon 98b, 99d, 100a, 100b. Where there is more than one photograph on a page,
credits follow the order in which they are referred to in the captions – a, b, c, etc.

Contents

Foreword

Because of filming commitments I could not get to Kiawah Island, but thanks to satellite television I was able to watch the 21 hours of coverage in Spain. I found it compulsive viewing and cannot praise the European side highly enough for the manner in which they competed and the graciousness they showed in defeat by the narrowest and cruellest of margins.

As a Scot, golf means a great deal to me. A true character builder, it tests not only your patience, but also your ability to handle pressure and I confess to feeling it from thousands of miles away, especially on that final day.

What pleased me particularly, too, was the way in which Bernard Gallacher, who comes from Bathgate not far from my own home city of Edinburgh and whom I have known for many years, handled what was for him a new and challenging role. His was a tough assignment but it seemed he grew in stature throughout the week.

I doubt whether I have seen more great shots hit, more clutch putts holed, more nail-biting drama and excitement than I saw at Kiawah and if there is the slightest chance of my being able to get to The Belfry in 1993 to see the next match, try and keep me away.

Congratulations again to the team that lost the Cup but won the admiration of so many for maintaining the game's well deserved and enviable record for good sportsmanship.

Sean Connery
Marbella 1991

1

Developing Goodwill

Over the years the Ryder Cup has meant a great deal to a great many people, not least Ben Hogan, Arnold Palmer and Jack Nicklaus, and of course myself. I looked forward to the biennial competition as eagerly in the days when I was a regular member of the side as Seve Ballesteros does today.

Apart from the World Matchplay, we golfers do not get too many opportunities to play head-to-head. Our golfing diet is usually with a card and pencil in medal competitions, where your score at every hole counts and you win by returning the lowest four-round aggregate, but in matchplay you might lose to an opponent whose overall score may be higher, but whose performance at a few key holes has been so good that you lose. Each hole is played individually. You win, halve or lose them. Matchplay is all about heart. A duel with golf clubs and not pistols. I have always loved it and the public, starved of it to a large extent, relish the opportunity to see the great players pitted against each other in the Ryder Cup every two years. I doubt we could handle the pressure of an annual Cup competition and, anyway, a biennial schedule not only gives the event a certain exclusivity, it ensures that when it does come round, everyone is eagerly looking forward to it – even more so now that it has become a match and we in Europe have the talent and the strength in depth to have the beating of the Americans. It was not always so. As European golf has boomed, so the Cup match has been given a new lease of life. This year for the first time I had the honour of captaining the team but, before turning to that, perhaps we should take a stroll back in history to remind ourselves when and how the Cup was started and how it has evolved into a golf event with an international reputation. It all began in the 1920s when golf in Britain and America was booming.

Like so many things in life, the Ryder Cup – watched these days by millions on television around the world – began casually enough. To be truthful, over tea at the Wentworth Club in Surrey where I am now the professional. To be strictly accurate, it was the future of the match which was assured at the tea party, when Samuel Ryder, a seed merchant from St Albans whose devotion to the game had stretched to his sponsorship of the stylish professional Abe Mitchell, agreed to put up a trophy for biennial competition between the professionals of America and Britain. It had not been Ryder's idea to stage the match. The driving force behind it had been inveterate golfing showman Walter Hagen, who had brought teams across to play in France and Britain in the years just after the First World War. The British had beaten Hagen's selection at Gleneagles in 1921 and when it was decided in 1926 that there should be pre-qualifying for the Open Championship that year, even for visiting Americans, Hagen hastily arranged a second challenge match. One of the qualifying courses was Sunningdale and it was logical that the match should take place at another excellent course in the vicinity – the West course at Wentworth.

After that match, which the British professionals handsomely won, Hagen, Mitchell and Ryder had tea together. Ryder had thoroughly enjoyed himself and had been particularly proud of the way Mitchell had played. He was in receptive mood when the question of a trophy to give the match a certain permanence was raised. Hagen had, in fact, tried to get an American friend to put up a trophy but nothing had come of it – not so much because the friend had lost interest, but rather that the matter had slipped his mind. The American's forgetfulness gave Samuel Ryder the opportunity to write himself indelibly into golfing history. A chance remark over tea and a sporting institution was born.

The trophy which Samuel Ryder in due course presented to the Professional Golfers' Association (PGA) is only 18 inches high but it is solid gold and has a style and grace about it that makes other golf trophies, especially the huge cups presented for competition in so many American events, look ostentatious. The figure on the lid is, appropriately, modelled on Abe Mitchell.

The significance of the Ryder Cup should not be overlooked. It gave a certain status to the professionals who, in those days, like the caddies, were considered inferior to the club members. Clubhouses were out of bounds on most occasions to the professionals and it was only through the efforts of Hagen and, in Britain, Henry (later Sir Henry) Cotton, that the professionals' status was improved.

These days there are two categories of golf professional – those who work permanently at a club and run the shop and tournament players who compete full time in competitions throughout Europe although often representing a club. A very few professionals, like me, have managed successfully to combine a club job with that of playing on Tour but we are in the minority. Back in the 1920s there was no such division or distinction. All professionals were club professionals. Those tournaments that were played finished on a Friday in order to let the contestants get back to their clubs and their members for the weekend. To have a trophy to play for every two years and the chance to travel abroad for the match every four years was a massive bonus – something to aim for.

Samuel Ryder's trophy did not instantly ensure the success of the biennial challenge. Indeed, Ryder had to pay the shortfall of £500 in the £3000 appeal launched by *Golf Illustrated* in 1927 to pay for the British team to travel to America for the first official match in June at Worcester, Massachusetts – a match which, ironically, Ryder's own man, Mitchell, was unable to attend because of illness. *Golf Illustrated* expected the money would be raised with ease but only 216 of the 1750 clubs in the British Isles supported the cause. The team was the first to represent Britain abroad in professional golf and had been selected by Harry Vardon, J. H. Taylor and James Braid, golf's Great Triumvirate. In an editorial published the day

11

before the team sailed from Southampton on board the *Aquitania* for New York, *Golf Illustrated* did not mince words: 'When we organised the Fund we hoped that the sportsmanship and patriotism of Britain's great army of golfers would enable three reserves to be sent as well in order to increase the chances of success. Sadly they have had to be left at home. The indifference and selfishness of the multitude of golfers to support this team is disappointing.'

Interest in the match in the United States, the magazine editor claimed, was considerable, but the depressing response to the appeal for money indicated that the golfers in Britain, although wishing to see British supremacy restored on the links, were too selfish to support the cause.

The list of donors to the fund was unusually varied. The Insurance Golfing Society of London had given 10 guineas. The members of South Herts Golf Club, whose professional in later years, Dai Rees, would captain one of the rare winning sides in 1957, donated seven guineas. An unnamed '18 handicapper' chipped in £6.00. The Vaudeville Golfing Society and the London Chemists' were among those pledging five guineas and a 'boy golfer' raided his 'piggy bank' to post off 2*s* 7*d*!

Many individuals sent donations as, of course, did golf clubs and golf unions, some of them from overseas. The Transvaal Golf Union clearly felt the Ryder Cup was a good idea by sending in a 10-guinea cheque! But if the response generally was disappointing, it only reflected the attitude most people had to all but a few professionals at the time. Still, with Samuel Ryder willingly dipping even deeper into the profits he was making from selling seeds to the public in penny packets, the team travelled, the match was played and a tradition was begun that is today stronger than ever.

Back in 1927 the PGA had the trophy and, by trust deed, the match all to itself, but the novelty of the event caused problems when the teams, minus Herbert Jolly, who went on another boat, arrived late after their seven-day transatlantic crossing. On arrival on 27 May, customs officials refused at first to let the British team take the trophy into the country although they later relented.

It had been a tiring journey and the team was ready for a quiet night on dry land but they were whisked off to a welcome dinner at the Westchester Biltmore Country Club, north of New York.

12

They had to sit through a vaudeville show and then, just when it seemed as if they might be able to slip quietly away, they were roped into a floodlit putting competition won by Aubrey Boomer. Britain won the putting competition but lost the match on 3 and 4 June convincingly enough, as did each of the visiting teams in the first of the four matches in the series. The problem was that not enough time was given to the team that had sailed the Atlantic to find their land legs again. Some players lost their rhythm and balance.

In 1927 the British did not want to attend the pre-match banquet, held the night before the match began, because it was felt that it might affect the team's preparation, but after discussions behind the scenes, they did attend. American Walter Hagen, however, true to character, turned up halfway through the meal.

There was even a move then to abandon the foursomes and substitute them with fourball matches but the British officials would have none of that. They felt the professional version of amateur golf's Walker Cup contest should be played along Walker Cup lines.

At Massachusetts, Britain promptly lost the foursomes 3–1 and the next day lost the singles series too. Only George 'miss 'em quick' Duncan, noted for the speed at which he putted, won. Charles Whitcombe and Gene Sarazen halved, but a pattern had been set.

13

The Americans were using only home-based players and the PGA in Britain decided to 'do the decent thing' and choose only British-based professionals, thus eliminating from selection, after 1929, British players such as Boomer, Henry Cotton and Percy Alliss who were based in continental Europe.

With hindsight it looks to have been a typical head-in-the-sand attitude from those charged with the task of running the match, a misguided effort to be fair to the Americans. Ironically, 50 years later the PGA, wisely wanting to save the match and make it more of a contest, jumped at the opportunity to bring in not just any continental-based Briton but any continental! Anyway, the Americans lost in 1929 at Moortown and Britain lost in 1931 at Scioto in Columbus, Ohio, where Jack Nicklaus would later play as a boy. That match was close. Britain won at Southport in 1933 and were well beaten in New Jersey in 1935, but the home-win pattern was shattered in the last Ryder Cup to be staged before the Second World War.

Walter Hagen, who had boasted that he had brought a winning side with him, captained America to an 8–4 victory again at Southport in June 1937. A desperately poor show in the foursomes was the reason given for the Southport debacle, according to correspondent Guy B. Farrar in a surprisingly candid report in *Golf Illustrated*. 'The Americans threw the foursomes at us with both hands and we just refused, with equal courtesy, to accept them,' he wrote.

The inability to play well in foursomes, still a problem at Kiawah in 1991, has dogged our Ryder Cup teams over the years. In 44 series of foursomes the British, then the British and Irish, and now the Europeans, have won only eight of them.

At the end of the Second World War there was the distinct chance that the match might not resume again because of lack of money. The war had taken its toll on British resources and even two years after hostilities had ended, there was no spare money to sponsor a team to play golf in America. There were doubts about the match being staged until an American Anglophile, Bob Hudson, imbued with the same spirit Samuel Ryder had shown 20 years earlier, stepped forward. He made the necessary arrangements to underwrite the team's expenses and took Henry Cotton and his men to Portland, Oregon, for a match against a powerful American squad, captained by Ben Hogan. Just how powerful that American team was, compared to the war-weary British, can be judged from the scoreline – United States 11, Great Britain and Ireland 1. Sam King, in the last singles, prevented the American whitewash with a 4 and 3 victory over Herman Keiser.

The next four matches went America's way. They won at Ganton in 1949, Pinehurst in 1951, Wentworth in 1953 and then at the Thunderbird Golf and Country Club in 1955, but the matches were not without controversy and drama.

In September 1949, Ben Hogan, captaining the American side, and still using sticks as he recovered from his appalling car accident of earlier in the year, complained about the potential illegality of some of the British players' clubs, especially the grooves on the face of Max Faulkner's wedge. This was a follow-up to Henry Cotton's having asked for the American clubs to be tested at Oregon two years earlier. Golf writer Bernard Darwin, a considerable figure in the game and the official referee, resolved the issue by commanding the players to sort it out like gentlemen. In the end, a little overnight filing of some of the club faces put everything right.

In 1957 there was something of a surprise at Lindrick Golf Club on the outskirts of Sheffield. Britain and Ireland won and deservedly so. Inevitably we lost the foursomes (1–3), but we then swept to glorious victory in the singles. Peter Alliss, playing third and with considerable credit against Fred Hawkins, lost his game but long before he had finished, Britain and Ireland had enough points on the board to ensure a first victory since 1933 and only the third home win since Samuel Ryder had presented the trophy. Reporter Tom Scott, always the master of understatement, was impressed enough to write that he had witnessed probably the most memorable few hours in the history of British golf. I wonder what he would think of the matches now.

The American captain, Jackie Burke, had asked Scott after the 1957 match: 'What happened?' The answer was simple enough – the Americans had not been able to control the smaller British ball (now, of course, the ball is a standard size around the world but it was not then) in the winds that had sprung up in the afternoon. Eric Brown took care of the fiery Tommy Bolt 4 and 3, Peter Mills was the 15th-green winner over American captain Burke, and then, in quick succession, Ken Bousfield, battling Dai Rees, stylish Bernard Hunt and supremely talented Christy O'Connor gave Britain and Ireland the points for a glorious victory.

'You won Eric, but I did not enjoy the game,' snarled Bolt after the match. 'No, of course you did not enjoy it,' replied the equally testy Brown, 'because you got licked.'

In 1959 the match at the Eldorado Country Club was notable for 'the long drop'. The British team were caught in a storm as they flew across the San Jacinto mountains from Los Angeles to Palm Springs and it took all the pilot's skill to avoid a crash as the plane, out of control, plummeted 4000 feet from its altitude of 13,000. With Dai Rees, Harry Weetman, John Jacobs, Christy O'Connor and Eric Brown among those on board, the frightening, near fatal incident was a front-page lead for the highly respected *Daily Express* reporter Ronald Heager. After the captain regained control of the battered plane they returned to Los Angeles and the team made

15

the journey the next day by bus! If the losing British team's collective nerve was slightly a-jangle on that occasion it was hardly surprising.

In 1961 the Americans came to Lytham and won and did so again by the comfortable margin of 23–9 at East Lake, Atlanta, two years later. In 1965 America won at Royal Birkdale by seven points and in 1967 we lost at Houston. Arnold Palmer was at the height of his popularity then but that cut no ice with team captain Hogan. That was the year when Palmer asked him if there were any truth that the Americans were going to be playing the smaller British ball in the match because he might not have any in his bag. Hogan stared him out: 'Who said that you are playing?'

The Ryder Cup match, in earlier times, never lacked spirited confrontation and there was bad blood spilled in 1969 at Royal Birkdale when Eric Brown had been entrusted to the captaincy of the side for the first time and I made my first appearance.

Let me digress for one moment because Eric Brown and I come from the same club, Bathgate. The course is squeezed in between a factory and a railway line some 25 miles from Edinburgh. Golf was a natural game for me to take up because my father was a keen player. I suppose there were signs early on that I was a better than average performer. As a teenager I competed on the local club circuit breaking course records every week. I played international golf for Scotland and for Britain and I won the Scottish Open Amateur title in 1967, emulating Eric who had long since left the club before I came along but whose reputation influenced me considerably.

During my amateur career I never played in the Walker Cup. I had turned professional before I had the chance to do so. I had appreciated the potential a career in golf offered me and did not want to lose a moment cashing in. Within a year I was the European No. 1, winning two titles in 1969, my second season and the year I made my Ryder Cup debut.

I never liked losing and in Ryder Cup terms I have taken on the best and beaten them. In 1969 I was a little disappointed when I was dropped by Eric for the morning singles – in those days there were two series of singles on the final day, not one. Eric told me that he wanted me to be fresh for a big challenge in the afternoon. What a challenge it proved to be. I found myself up against the

1968 US Open champion, Lee Trevino, whom Maurice Bembridge and I had beaten in the first series of foursomes. The exuberant Trevino had beaten the stylish Peter Alliss in the morning singles but in the afternoon I surprised some people, but not myself, by beating the much more experienced American 4 and 3.

The 1969 match produced the first draw of the series with Jack Nicklaus – not completely to the delight of his captain, smooth-swinging but tough-as-nails Sam Snead – conceding Tony Jacklin's final putt to ensure that the honours were even (16–16) at the end. Tony won three and halved two of his five games and was as inspirational to the side on the course as he would prove to be off it when he captained the side in the 1980s.

The Cup competition that year had been a tense, bad-tempered affair with the American, Ken Still, making himself particularly unpopular, maybe as a result of his intense desire to help America fight back from a surprising two-point deficit after the first two foursomes and one of the fourball series. Still and Dave Hill had been drawn to play against Brian Huggett and me and on the 7th hole Huggett suggested Still had putted out of turn. An incensed Still, after an angry exchange, picked up his ball, conceding the hole in the most impolite manner. At the next, the still seething Still, who had not endeared himself to the crowd in earlier games, claimed the hole from us on a petty pretext and the crowd let him know how they felt.

17

Dai Rees, one of the officials that year, tried to cool things down but there was nearly a punch-up. By the 9th the crowd were chanting 'Stay out' when Still putted. It was not what Samuel Ryder, who had been so impressed by the manner in which the 1926 match at Wentworth had been played, would have wanted, but the incident does underline how great the commitment to the match has always been.

Over the years I have been involved in many memorable matches, including one at Old Warson Country Club in 1971 against my opposite number at Kiawah, Dave Stockton. Stockton was at the height of his playing career and remembers how well he did to hole the 15-footer on the last to hold me to a halved game. We lost the match but I did have the satisfaction of beating Charles Coody in the tremendous heat and humidity of St Louis, Missouri.

There was more trouble on the course that year, caused this time by Gardner Dickinson, and I was involved in it. In the fourballs Peter Oosterhuis and I were playing Dickinson and Arnold Palmer. At the short 7th hole, a 207-yard hole where the green was elevated and the tee shot blind, Palmer played and received a tremendous ovation for what we reckoned was a 5-iron shot that finished pin-high. As I stepped on to the tee to play my shot with a 3-iron, my caddie, an American, casually asked Palmer's caddie what Arnold had hit. The question, while illegal, had no bearing on the club I was using. I heard neither the question nor the answer. I was busy lining up my shot and subsequently hit my ball inside Palmer's. The hole was halved in 3 but Dickinson then claimed it, because we had broken Rule 9 which states that a player or his caddie cannot ask for advice from the opposition or their caddies. In this case, my caddie had asked Palmer's caddie a question. The referee had no option but to give it to them although Palmer tried to reverse the ruling. The Americans then went on to win by 5 and 4.

Hit by food poisoning in 1973 at Muirfield on the only occasion that the match was played in Scotland, I lost out in the singles to Tom Weiskopf, who had won the Open Championship that year at Troon. The Americans won by six points but we gave them a considerable fright, leading by 5½ to 3½ after the first day. The American captain that year was again Jackie Burke, hoping to gain some revenge for his defeat in 1957 when the playing captain.

Two years later I halved with Trevino and with Al Geiberger at Arnold Palmer's cosy Laurel Valley Club high in the Pennsylvania mountains at Ligonier. Laurel Valley was close to the Latrobe Club where Arnold Palmer had learned the game but which he now owns. Taking the match there indicated how much respect the PGA of America had for Arnold. Yet by going to such an out-of-the-way spot, where the crowds were inevitably going to be small, it underlined, too, how casually the PGA of America approached the match.

The Ryder Cup at this time was not a money spinner. Indeed, the fixture had been left with the PGA of America when the US Tour had been formed as a breakaway organization in 1968. The match was not seen then as an 'earner' and I suppose the Tour players may well be sorry that they gave the match over to the PGA so easily. Compared with today there was little or no hype in 1975 when the Laurel Valley match was played.

It was highlighted for us by Jack Nicklaus losing twice to big Brian Barnes, but the Americans won by 10 points and the Cup as a spectacle and a contest was again in danger of being shelved. The Americans had won all but two of the 16 meetings since 1947 and there seemed little prospect of the match becoming more competitive.

It was mooted that Commonwealth players might be used to strengthen the British side but all that was done for 1977 was to change the format, reducing the points availability in order to dilute America's strength in depth. There were huge gaps between the games at Lytham and the format was hardly a success with the Americans who felt it was a long way to come to play for just 20 points.

Despite all the pressure, I have never felt too nervous at Cup matches and I suppose one of my most pleasant memories of 1977 was of beating Jack Nicklaus in a game that looked like being a nightmare for me. Minutes before I was scheduled to tee off my putter disappeared from my bag and I had to acquire another from the professional's shop. Despite the upset, I don't know how or why but I was very calm on the 1st tee as I prepared to take on the man most regard as the greatest of all golfers.

19

Nicklaus never knew what hit him. I won the first four holes. The home crowd loved it and enjoyed it until Nicklaus, as expected, fought back, chipping away at my lead until we were all-square with two to play. Now something extra was required and I managed to find it in the shape of an 80-foot putt which snaked across the green and into the hole to win the 17th. I won the point by halving the last under the most severe pressure, but then that is the thrill you get from playing the game at the highest level.

Nick Faldo will not forget that week either, because he made a spectacular debut, much encouraged and helped by experienced Peter Oosterhuis in fourball and foursomes matches and gaining a point in the penultimate game in the singles against Tom Watson, who was at his peak. The overall result, however, was the same, the Americans won. The crisis regarding the future of the Ryder Cup was now acute. New blood needed to be found to increase our competitiveness. In 1976 a young Spaniard, Severiano Ballesteros, had almost won the Open and continental golfers were beginning to make their presence felt on the newly constituted European Tour which John Jacobs, and later Ken Schofield, had set up with Tony Jacklin. It was logical that the continentals (i.e. the talented Ballesteros) would be asked to join in and for the British and Irish side to become a European one. Fifteen years before official European economic union, golf blazed the European trail. The suggestion of such a change came to Lord Derby, then our president, from Jack Nicklaus and others in America. Nicklaus had written saying that, while realizing that national pride was involved, reality must prevail if the event was not going to decline into little more than a formality and especially if it was to remain a vital part of the US golf calendar. The Cup match was worth preserving and how wise it was in the late 1970s to move with the times.

Ballesteros and Antonio Garrido were the first continentals in the European side against the Americans at Sam Snead's old haunt, The Greenbrier, at White Sulphur Springs in West Virginia, another American venue guaranteed to ensure the match, albeit now against Europe, had a certain exclusivity. I gave Lanny Wadkins his first Cup defeat in that match but the Americans still won and turned up at Walton Heath two years later with probably the strongest side ever brought together. It was headed by Tom Watson and Jack Nicklaus who was to be playing for the last time. I halved with Open champion Bill Rogers, but the game that made the headlines was the one in which Tom Kite beat Sandy Lyle 3 and 2. Kite was 10 under par, Lyle six under at the finish. Birdies in that game were more prominent than pars. The Americans romped home winners by 11 points, but the tide was turning. Since then the matches have been desperately close.

I had played in seven matches and, for me, there was one more to come. In 1983 at Palm Beach Gardens the Americans won by a point after a match which underlined the new-found confidence of the Europeans, especially those playing regularly in the United States such as Faldo, Lyle, Langer and Ballesteros. Why I remember the match so well was that the overall result was dependent on the last game between Tom Watson and myself. Watson won the 17th after I, with the adrenalin pumping, had sent my tee shot through the green into the clinging fringe grass. Watson also missed the green but, believing he would make 3, I tried to be too clever with my recovery and in the end lost the hole to a bogey 4 and the game 2 and 1. US captain Nicklaus never looked more relieved. He sweated more there that week than he has during most of his major triumphs, aware, as I would find out too, that he had no control over what his players were doing on the course.

The Belfry had not been ready for the 1981 Cup match which had to be switched to Walton Heath, but it was in 1985 when the Europeans won back the Cup magnificently. Sam Torrance had the pleasure of holing the winning putt and we won the final series of singles to underline our superiority over the three days. It was Europe 16½, United States 11½. Twenty-eight years had passed since our last victory at Lindrick and the scenes of jubilation were remarkable and memorable. Tony Jacklin and his team had restored our pride and there was the additional bonus for him of having led a European side to victory over a team captained by Lee Trevino, the man who had denied him his second Open Championship title at Muirfield in 1972. Sunday 15 September 1985 was, according to Jacklin, the day that European golf came of age. The Americans were, frankly, stunned.

Just to prove that what had happened at The Belfry was no flash in the pan we went to Jack Nicklaus's own course, Muirfield Village, in 1987 and won again. Jack led the American team once more and was confident of winning the trophy back, but on his own course he created a dubious slice of Cup history by becoming the first American captain to lose on home soil. It was Europe's first away win and they did so on a course that the Americans knew better and on which they were expected to play better.

As it was, the Europeans played as magnificently as they had in 1985, maybe even better. After two days they led 10½ to 5½ and needed only another four points out of the remaining 12 singles for overall victory. The European support for our team was magnificent that year, so much so that Jack Nicklaus had to recruit fans in the hope that they might inspire his team in the way our fans were inspiring us. They did not.

That year the romantic hero was Ireland's Eamonn Darcy who had been one down to Ben Crenshaw with two to play but gained a precious point. A precision-perfect 6-iron ensured a winning birdie at the 17th for the popular Irishman with the eccentric swing from Delgany, near Dublin. That squared the match and after gentle Ben had driven into a ditch at the last, Eamonn was left with a downhill, five-foot, left-to-right-breaking putt for a vital point at an important stage in the match when the Europeans, up against it in the singles, needed a morale booster. Darcy became part of Ryder Cup legend when he holed to win his game. Later he was carried shoulder-high through the tented village area when the European team and their vocal supporters celebrated well into the night.

The victory dinner was a subdued affair. Jack Nicklaus, like Jackie Burke in 1957, would have been forgiven for asking Tony, 'What happened?' Europe's players had emphasized they were no longer the golfing underdogs to the Americans who had been inclined to think of their 1985 defeat as just a rogue result. Led by Nicklaus they had failed to win the Cup back. They may not have been able to see much of the match live on that occasion because American television had not yet discovered the Cup, but golfers all round the United States were beginning to realize American golfing supremacy had been shattered.

The Ryder Cup match, which had for so long been an opportunity for the officials of both Britain and America to get together every two years to discuss mutual matters while the players competed on the course, had become a more serious, competitive affair. The match had taken on new meaning. The Americans realized that Samuel Ryder's Cup was worth trying to get back.

In 1989 the match was again held at the Belfry and for only the second time in Cup history ended in a tie. Golf was the real winner said American captain Raymond Floyd, who felt so confident about his team's chances that he told President George Bush at a pre-match White House lunch that he would bring the Cup back. Was he red-faced? Of course he did not keep his promise. The Europeans kept the Cup by drawing a match they might have won but had looked to have lost until Christy O'Connor Jnr, a wild card this time after having been passed over by Tony Jacklin in 1985, hit a career 2-iron shot to the large three-tiered last green to beat Fred Couples. Ronan Rafferty, Jose Maria Canizares, Jose Maria Olazabal and Mark James ensured the draw but the Americans rallied, winning the last four points, with Curtis Strange winning the last four holes brilliantly against the European anchor man, Ian Woosnam.

When the sides had drawn in 1969 we shared the Cup, each side holding it for a year. Twenty years later there was no such offer from the Europeans. The message was simple. The Americans would have to win the Cup back. Two years later at Kiawah Island, the greatest golfers of the world would meet again in fair and honest competition and I was persuaded, not unwillingly, to take on the job everyone loves when the team is winning. I had been given the honour of leading the side.

2

Off Course
Battles

I played in my last Ryder Cup match in 1983 at Palm Beach Gardens in Florida. In 1969 in the singles at Royal Birkdale, in my first Cup appearance, I had been pitched in against Trevino and won. In my last game I was in the anchor role against Tom Watson. I had not been fully fit that week. I had played and practised little and captain Tony Jacklin, no doubt, expected to have the match won by the time I finished. But he knew I was a fighter and put me in the anchor role. In the end I didn't win and the team lost by a point. One journalist cruelly suggested that for me it had been one match too many. I don't think it was: I just lost, but I knew I had played for the last time.

I had played continuously since making my debut at Royal Birkdale and Tony was kind enough to write to me in 1985, when as I had anticipated I did not earn a place in the side, saying that it would seem strange to be playing a Ryder Cup without my being around. He felt I had something to offer. Would I be prepared to go and help him? In actual fact I was on the Ryder Cup committee at the time and would have been at the match in an official capacity anyway, but I jumped at the chance of maintaining a closer connection with a fixture which, over the years, had become so important to me.

Anyone who knows Tony Jacklin knows that he is his own man and runs his own show. When he had been approached to take over the captaincy two years earlier by Ken Schofield, the executive director of the PGA European Tour, Tony had laid down the ground rules for his acceptance. These included the upgrading of the whole Ryder Cup operation, not least the travel. He wanted the team to go to America in 1983 feeling they were the equals of the Americans, not the poor relations. To do that, he felt, required a major change in attitude by the PGA. He got the fullest cooperation. The team flew to Florida by Concorde and the closeness of the result at the PGA National course justified his insistence that if we were going to beat the Americans – and we had not done so since 1957 – we must not go into the match as inferiors. Our best man, Seve Ballesteros, was equal to or even better than their best, and the next three in line – Nick Faldo, Bernhard Langer and Sandy Lyle – could more than hold their own with the toughest of the Americans. The Americans still had the strength in depth, however, although the gap was narrowing all the time.

Tony knew how he wanted to run the show and what my role would be. I was to drive him around in the electric buggy and talk to him, keep him informed. He had always enjoyed having someone around to use as a sounding board, someone to bounce ideas off. He needed someone whose opinions he respected and, happily, I fitted the bill. We were both on the same wavelength, sometimes, uncannily, being able to read each other's minds and assess situations instantly. At the time I remember one newspaper suggesting that I had been appointed as Tony's minder, a reference to the television series in which Dennis Waterman acted as minder to George Cole, but that comparison would be stretching it. I was just an aide-de-camp, a helper, someone to whom he or a player could turn if he wanted something done. In 1989, for instance, Sam Torrance had needed a fresh supply of carrots to chew as he played round. He liked them, wanted them, and I got them delivered to him.

It is amazing how many things can go wrong at a Ryder Cup. When our golf bags were delivered to Muirfield Village, in 1987, we were surprised to find that they were the wrong size. How did

25

it happen? I will never know, but it was my job to get Titleist to change them double-quick and supervise the printing of the names of the players on the new bags in time for the first foursomes series. This was a chore that the captain would not have wanted while he was working with his team to get them psychologically ready for the match. When I took over the captaincy I asked Spain's Manuel Pinero to do the same for me at Kiawah Island. Manuel was experienced, had played in two Ryder Cups, knew the players, and was utterly reliable. I knew from understudying Tony that, when the match starts, the captain needs to clear his mind of everything except what is happening in the match, and believe me, that is tough. Without help it would be impossible. I like to think too that by just being around Tony in 1985, 1987 and 1989 and discussing possible pairings I stimulated discussion and threw in a few ideas which helped him make the difficult final decisions.

Instinct plays an important part in all this and Tony had it. His decision in 1983 to play Seve with rookie Paul Way was a gamble but it paid off, even if Seve complained that he was having to act as a father figure. Tony asked Seve to do a job and, like a good team man, he did it and the unusual partnership won 2½ points out of 4. I certainly enjoyed my role with Tony, though it hardly matched up to the excitement I had felt as a player when stepping on to the tee against Lee Trevino, Jack Nicklaus or Tom Watson, not just to play for myself but for my country and latterly for Europe. Tony was having such success that many of us thought that he would go on for a few more matches before retiring. He seemed set to lead the side more times than even Dai Rees, who had captained the team on five occasions. He had earned the tremendous respect of the team and clearly relished his role, even if he did lose weight every two years during Cup week as a direct result of the stress that captaincy entailed. The rewards of victory, however, or the satisfaction in the nail-biting draw that had enabled us to keep the Cup in 1989, made all the stomach-churning tension that went with the job more bearable.

I suppose it was no surprise that I was being talked about as Tony's natural successor when he indicated that he would be stepping down following the second successful defence of the Cup. Yet I had never thought seriously about lobbying for the post when he gave it up,

26

for several good reasons. I knew that if I took the job I would have
to work closely with the press, radio and television, and I have never
been completely at ease in this field. I am a very private person and
I could envisage that as captain I would have to adopt a much more
public persona. I knew too that the captaincy would affect my wife,
Lesley, and family because of the additional demands it would make
on me in the months leading up to the event. If this seems strange,
you must remember that I turned professional as a teenager and
have been in the public eye for over 20 years. There comes a time
when you want, quite simply, to drop out of the limelight and I
understood that this would not be possible if I became captain.
Although I felt I had the experience to do the job and had no reservations about handling the players and the competitive side of the
match, I did have serious reservations about the other aspects of
the post, especially as I knew I would be taking over from the most
successful of captains at a most difficult time.

The major problem was the ongoing dispute, battle, argument,
call it what you will, between the PGA European Tour, the tournament players' division which provides the players for the match,
and the PGA, the club professionals' organization to whom Samuel
Ryder had presented the Cup in 1927 and to whom he had entrusted
the staging of the biennial competition. Although Tony Jacklin and
his teams had been doing brilliantly on the course, there was still
a major difference of opinion in the respective boardrooms about
how the new-found profits from the Ryder Cup, which had run for
so long at a loss, should be split up. Yet despite all that, I readily
took the job when it was offered.

27

I thought that I might be able to bring the two factions together
more quickly and end the arguments which I considered were damaging the reputation of them both. I found out quickly enough that
neither I nor Lord Derby, who was in the unique position of being
president of both the PGA and the PGA European Tour, would be
able to effect a quick reconciliation. The issue would come to a
head in the most public way months later and I would be right in
the middle of it.

The problem stemmed from the time the Tour players had split
away from the PGA to form a separately financed division in the
early 1970s. The two bodies were now operating independently,

but the decision in 1979 to embrace the continentals in the Ryder Cup brought the Tour and the PGA together again officially. The British PGA, even with the continentals in the side, were determined, however, to hang on to the match by squeezing the European Tour out of the organization and out of the potential profit split. They felt it was their Cup, their match, and it was not for sale, but I knew the players would not stand for that.

I have never been able to understand why Lord Derby, as chairman of the joint Ryder Cup committee, did not realize the damaging consequences of a prolonged dispute and nip the issue in the bud early on. He could have forced both sides to sit down and thrash out a mutually satisfactory commercial arrangement: both divisions needed each other to keep the match alive. No player wanted to see a great fixture such as the Ryder Cup killed off as a result of internal bickering, least of all me, but I knew too that the situation was serious. As far as I was concerned the bottom line had always been that the PGA needed the money more than the players needed the PGA, but that the Cup match could only continue if both sides reached a sensible, simple and essentially equal business agreement. What was clear, except to the PGA, was that the players were not making a takeover bid for the Ryder Cup. All the players wanted was a properly arranged partnership. Because of the facts I had available to me as a member of the joint Ryder Cup comittee, chaired by Lord Derby and comprising three representatives from the Tour and three from the PGA, I was aware that, looking at the situation from the worst possible perspective, there might not be another match. It was that bad back in 1989.

Immediately after the Cup had been retained at The Belfry, both Seve Ballesteros and outgoing captain Jacklin had said publicly that I should be offered the job, but I felt at the time that the PGA were not wildly enthusiastic about my taking over. They knew that I was strongly aligned towards the Tour, just as Tony had been, and the PGA had, shall I say, 'gone off him a bit'. As long as they saw Tony as neutral they were happy enough, but when he put his cards on the table and supported the Tour on the issue of profit sharing they were suspicious. The difficulty in which I found myself was not made any easier by the fact that former PGA captain and chairman, Peter Alliss, whose views are so respected by millions on television,

28

felt the need to take up the cudgels on behalf of the PGA by strongly opposing the views of Jacklin, Ballesteros and, in some respects, me. We all wanted a partnership but Alliss's view was that the PGA should retain full and total control of the match against what he imagined was the threat of a Tour takeover.

In fact, far from wanting to prise the match away from the PGA, the Tour was so well aware of the importance that the profit from the Cup played in meeting the annual costs and growth of the PGA's administration, that an offer was made to the PGA: the Tour, while retaining the television revenues, which they saw as part of their overall BBC deal on tournaments, would not split the profits until £750,000 had been placed in the PGA funds. The figure was not reached casually. It was what the PGA considered they required to finance their operation during non-Ryder Cup years or when the match was being played in America and was therefore not directly earning money for the PGA. The retention of the TV revenue by the Tour was counterbalanced by the PGA retaining the special tax concession the Tour had not enjoyed since the breakaway and did not want.

As if all that ongoing controversy was not a bizarre enough scenario, there was the vexed issue of the venue for the 1993 match, scheduled to be played on this side of the Atlantic. I felt that the Spanish players, especially Seve, had had such a tremendous impact on the modern success of the Cup that Spain deserved to stage the match in 1993, as long as certain provisos were met. The PGA had been very happy to change the rules in 1979 in order to give us the chance to field Seve at a time when the Ryder Cup was in danger of dying; but not enough thought had been given to the obvious implications of what expanding into Europe really meant.

Seve's commitment to the Ryder Cup since 1983, when Tony Jacklin had persuaded him to play again after he had been left out in 1981, has remained consistently strong. Tony had been passed over in 1981, too, and while he had realized that the game and the match were bigger than any one individual, he had had to persuade Seve to change his mind about never again playing in the match. I was well aware of the role Seve had played, not just in the Cup matches but in making the Volvo-sponsored PGA European Tour what it is today, so I felt comfortable about supporting a move to

29

take the match to Spain at a time when Seve would still be able to play in the side.

Providing the match could be guaranteed to make as much profit as it would were it staged in Britain, and providing a suitable course could be found, I felt – and so did the Tour – that it was a way of acknowledging Seve's contribution to the game and of recognizing Spain as the main growth area of the Tour. There was a great deal of argument about the possible venue, Club de Campo, close to the heart of Madrid. There were problems about it, I know, but these were never really looked into thoroughly. When we decided to go to The Belfry for the first time in 1981, we couldn't do so because the course was not ready. Who was to say that changes, albeit major changes, could not have been made at Club de Campo in time for 1993? Failing that, a new course could have been completed near the Spanish capital. There was time: the Kiawah Ocean course was still being seeded and laid out 18 months before the match took place there in 1991. A hurricane had gone through the area of South Carolina causing considerable devastation and delayed Kiawah, but it was ready when the time came and Spain, I felt, could have been ready in 1993. The bottom line was that the Tour's idea of going to Spain was turned down out of hand.

I always felt that the British public were against the idea of the Ryder Cup being moved away from Britain. The British golf fan is quite happy to have the Cup match played here every four years and sees no reason to switch it, even though we now play under the EC flag. The Ryder Cup argument to them is similar to the attitude so many have regarding the Common Market. People are all for it, as long as they are getting something out of it, but they turn against it when they have to put something in. I suspect the PGA sensed this and relied on the public being on their side, but I was disappointed that the PGA did not support the Tour on the Spanish issue.

With so much controversy surrounding the Ryder Cup, you can understand why I was nervous about accepting the captaincy, proud though I was to have been given the chance. I remained worried that if the split between the two bodies got any deeper the PGA might nominate another captain of their own and not accept me, despite the fact that I was the nominee of the Tour and had

30

had the appointment ratified by the Ryder Cup committee. Although the Tour felt that the joint committee was charged with the task of supervising arrangements for the Cup, the PGA were, I believe, of the increasingly firm view that in the final analysis the responsibility belonged to them and that all Ryder Cup committee decisions should be further ratified by them. This, in their opinion, extended as well to the captaincy. When Tony Jacklin had been chosen as captain in 1983 it was the tournament committee of the PGA European Tour who selected him and their nomination was then rubber-stamped by the Ryder Cup committee. In other words the players who were going to form the team were, in effect, choosing the man to lead them. It should have happened that way again in 1989 but my appointment became part of the larger power struggle.

I could see the way the PGA were thinking: if the players were allowed to choose the captain, that was an indication that they were not in sole charge. It seemed to me that John Lindsey, the executive director of the PGA, and the chairman, Philip Weaver, wanted to extend PGA control over the match to the choosing of the captain. In fact, a few names other than my own were being bandied around as potential captains when I was asked by Lindsey and Weaver to meet them at the Manchester Trade Show.

This meeting took place in November 1989, before the scheduled Tour meeting at which they both knew I would be confirmed as the players' choice to captain the team. I was suspicious about their motives for asking me to go to Manchester because I was worried about the central issue of who would have the right to choose the captain, the players or the PGA. We met in a public restaurant and after discussing the matter for some time I got the distinct impression that they felt obliged to go along with my appointment. Among the various topics raised was, rather curiously, the person whom I would appoint as my vice captain, a role that I had filled for Tony in every respect but name.

The PGA officials seemed to put great importance on the appointment of a vice captain, despite the fact that there had not been one in the past. Spain's Manuel Pinero was a name they mentioned at the time. I indicated that rather than have a vice captain, I would want to operate in the same way as Tony who had had the

31

support of quite a few players, of whom I had been just one. As the discussion continued I realized that the PGA's real concern was the possibility that whomsoever I chose as my right-hand man – maybe even a Spaniard – would get the nomination later from the players to be my successor.

At that meeting I conceded no ground, gave way on no issue and in the end they could not have been in any doubt that they were dealing with someone who was always going to fight hard for the right of the players to choose the captain and who, on the wider issues, was of the view that the Ryder Cup should be a partnership. When I left the meeting to fly back to London, I knew the PGA officials were going to agree to my being appointed and that their support would avoid a constitutional mess which would have deepened the rift between the two sides and endangered even more the future of the Cup. That at least was gratifying.

I told no one else about the Manchester meeting, not even Ken Schofield or the tournament committee, because I knew how mad they would have been at what was happening. I was interested in bringing the two groups closer together and believed that it served everyone's best interest to say nothing. What the PGA had done to me had not been particularly pleasant. After all, it was not as if I was an unknown. I had played my heart out on eight Ryder Cup teams. I had been on Tour for 20 years and served on the tournament committee and the boards of both the PGA and the Tour at separate times. I felt there had been little need for them to invite me anywhere to look me over.

A few weeks later I was nominated, as expected, by the players to do the job and my appointment was ratified by the Ryder Cup committee. Yet I was still worried that, despite all that had been said at the Manchester meeting, nothing was absolutely certain until a proper business agreement had been signed by the two bodies. This concern was not eased by the delay in announcing that I had got the job. All of my colleagues knew that I was the nominee and it was beginning to be an embarrassment as people kept asking whether or not I had in fact been given the post. Eventually I forced the issue and an announcement was made between Christmas and the New Year to end the uncertainty.

At least I was now seen to have been appointed but despite the

Tour bending over backwards to get an agreement, there was still nothing signed between the Tour and the PGA. It was a crazy situation. The only way that we were going to achieve a permanent and lasting solution was for the matter to reach breaking point, with the inevitable chance of casualties. As it was, there was a casualty in the early summer of 1990 when Lord Derby resigned as president of the Tour after siding with the PGA on the choice of the 1993 venue.

That meeting was held at Wentworth during the Volvo PGA Championship. The Tour had made their situation quite clear and I reinforced the view when asked to go on BBC Television during the week of the Benson & Hedges International at St Mellion in April to talk about the Cup match and my job.

Interviewer Steve Rider had quizzed me about the controversy regarding the next venue and pointed out that even the players were arguing amongst themselves about it. Seve wanted Spain for obvious reasons, Bernhard Langer had suggested that Portmarnock might be the best venue, Nick Faldo favoured a more traditional seaside venue in Britain such as Royal Birkdale. The arguments had become quite heated at times, with Seve creating the wrong kind of headlines at the Spanish Open in Madrid when he suggested Nick keep his mouth shut about the venue and stick to playing golf!

In my reply to Steve Rider I said, with the full authority of the Tour, that the three men on the Ryder Cup committee representing the Tour would be recommending a Spanish venue in 1993. I was careful to stress that it was a recommendation, and I repeated that view in the press tent later. My interview caused much concern. PGA executive director, John Lindsey, criticized me for speaking out before the meeting and Peter Alliss had quite a lot to say on the subject as well as disagreeing with any suggestion that the match should go to the continent.

The way we saw it, the Tour had come clean on the issue. We had shown the officials in Spain that they had our support and, more importantly, we had indicated to the PGA the way we were thinking in order to avoid a potentially damaging stalemate when the Ryder Cup committee met to decide the venue. What prompted us to go public was the fact that we could not get the PGA to reply to our request for informal discussions on the venue before the offi-

33

cial meeting. Letters requesting an official discussion to find common ground had gone unanswered. In hindsight I have no regrets in saying what I did, coming as it did at the end of a protracted one-sided negotiation with the PGA.

When we arrived for the meeting at Wentworth, Lord Derby came down on us like a ton of bricks, saying that we had embarrassed him and been discourteous to him as chairman by indicating our preference publicly. His reaction took me by surprise. I had spoken to him just after the BBC interview, stressing to him that the Tour's decision to vote for Spain was not a hard-and-fast one and that for the match to go to Madrid in 1993 we would still have to win the argument at the Ryder Cup committee meeting. He didn't think that I had done anything wrong and indicated this in a letter, yet when it came to that full meeting Lord Derby had changed his attitude. All we had been trying to do was to prevent our president from being put in the situation of having to use his casting vote.

We were halfway through the meeting before we realized that the block recommendation of the PGA was for The Belfry, for a third time. Inevitably, the vote would be 3–3. This came as a big shock to us as we thought the Tour had fulfilled all their contractual obligations to the Midland venue by having been there twice. We felt the Cup should be moved around and we were not in favour of a return. The PGA were not interested in compromise. Lord Derby, voting with them instead of adjourning the meeting to allow for further discussion, had little option but to resign as president of the PGA European Tour, the one thing we had been trying to avoid.

So I had been appointed and the venue of the 1993 match had been fixed, but there was still no binding business agreement between the two sides. The sorry business had dragged on long enough. I telephoned Ken Schofield to suggest that, in order to bring matters to a head, maybe it would be best if I resigned the captaincy. This would let the PGA choose their own captain if that was the way that they wanted to go. I was persuaded, however, that this would be quite the wrong course of action: it would be best for all of us to persevere despite all the problems and to keep trying to negotiate a proper business deal with the PGA. The long term

34

future of the march was paramount.

As the summer dragged on without agreement I got more depressed about the situation. Twice we had been close to settlement only for the PGA to renege and nothing had been signed by the time of the PGA Cup match in September 1990. The venue was Kiawah Island, not the Ocean course where the Ryder Cup was going to be played but Turtle Point, another of the courses on the complex. It had been suggested that I join the PGA party for the match in order to have a look at the Ryder Cup venue, still under construction.

I gave the matter considerable thought before deciding to accept.

3

Controversial Kiawah

If we had problems about the venue for the 1993 match, they had difficulties in America about where to stage it in 1991. The PGA of America had signed a deal with the Landmark Corporation to take the match to PGA West, the Pete Dye designed course in California where they hold the American Skins each year. Then in 1989 it was realized that because of the eight-hour time difference between there and London the match would become late-night and early-morning viewing for golf fans in Europe. It was decided to look for an alternative Landmark venue on the east coast of America. There were only two to choose from, Palm Beach Polo in Orlando, Florida, or the Ocean course at Kiawah Island, which architect Pete Dye had been commissioned to construct on a strip of land unsuitable for housing between the Atlantic Ocean and swampy marshland. Dye at first had not been keen on the idea but when he realized that he could build a course with several of the holes running along the seashore, unusual these days with such a premium on ocean frontage for luxury housing, he changed his mind.

Although there could be a crowd-control problem at what was

a comparatively remote venue, and despite the fact that the building schedule was incredibly tight with the match at that time only two years away, it was decided to gamble on Kiawah. Assuming all went well and the course was ready in time, the publicity factor for the new resort would be considerable. If all else failed they could use one of the three other existing courses on the island anyway!

As part of the PGA of America deal with Landmark it had been agreed that the PGA Cup match, the biennial competition between the club professionals of America and Europe, would be played in late 1990 at Kiawah on Turtle Point and, as Ryder Cup captain, I had been invited to join the official PGA party. Ideally I would have preferred to go to Kiawah on a low-key visit but I found myself roped into a full-scale American press day entitled 'One year to count down'. The hype had begun even then.

There had been some who had queried the appointment by Joe Walser, a former professional and senior vice president of Landmark, of Pete Dye to build the Ocean course. He is noted for designing tough courses. His aim, he says, is always to produce a finished product that will test the professional to the limit and this, I suppose, had to be the criteria for the Ryder Cup match. When you have the best 12 players in America and the best 12 in Europe battling it out you want them to be tested on a course which will examine all their skills. For Dye it was a challenge he could not refuse – a golden opportunity to do something no other architect had had the chance to do: to build a course on a prime slice of ocean-front real-estate without having to thread the holes around and through the houses.

Dye is unconventional in his approach. He is a former insurance man who made such a success of his self-financed first course – Crooked Stick in Indiana where John Daly won the 1991 USPGA Championship – that he turned to golf-course design and construction with no formal training in agronomy or engineering. His modus operandi is an unusual one. Whereas Jack Nicklaus has a team of highly skilled designers working with him and much of the work is done on the drawing board, Dye has no elaborate plans prepared. He does not work off blueprints. Instead, he goes to the site and lives there until the work has been completed to his satisfaction. He maintains that by living on site he can assess the conditions

37

in which the golfers will be playing and tailor the course to the prevailing weather patterns. Because he is a hands-on designer, there are comparatively few Dye-designed courses around. Even so, 10 of his courses are listed in the top 100 published by American magazines, *Golf Digest* and *Golf*.

The Ocean course, stretching some three miles, is situated on the north-eastern tip of a 10,000-acre barrier of sand. 'If I cannot build a great course here then I should be shot,' he told Walser, then added, 'and if you don't let me build it I'll shoot you!' Dye has always been influenced by Britain's seaside links, notably those in Scotland. He loves Scotland and wanted the course to look Scottish even if he was not able to produce a true Scottish links in South Carolina because the weather conditions are so different and the grasses that grow in Britain would not grow in that part of America. It would not be a seaside links but it would look like one.

The environment and ecology lobby is strong in the United States. Dye had to work to strict guidelines to protect the local animal and plant life but he was allowed to excavate irrigation lagoons and move sand around, except those primary dunes which fronted the beach and on which even spectators were not allowed to walk. I'm told that he did take a chance and move, usually in the late evening, some plants – especially sea oats – which he should not have done, but they flourished so well in their new environment in the rough alongside the fairways of the new course that no objections were raised. It is a tribute to Dye that, when the course was finished, all the wishes and demands of the environmentalists had been met.

Much of the course is artificially built up between the ocean and the swamp – built up more than Dye had originally planned in response to a remark by his wife Alice who suggested that it would be nice if, while playing the course, the golfers always had a view of the sea. Dye made the necessary adjustments and anyone who plays the course can only be delighted at Mrs Dye's brilliant idea. Whatever you think of the Ocean course it is panoramically spectacular.

Not only did Dye satisfy the environmental requirements, he also created something at the Ocean course that still has the experts baffled. He installed a unique internal drainage system that recycles water while protecting the adjacent marshland, or wetlands as they are called, from the necessary pesticides and herbicides used in golf greenkeeping. I was interested to hear how it works. A series of drains and 14 miles of underground pipes collect water falling on tees, greens, fairways and cart-paths and channel it into the irrigation system to be recycled. Even if the marsh with its alligators is only three feet away from the edge of the course, all the water that falls on the course is drained back into 22 acres of catchment basins and lagoons. There is no seepage and the wild life is protected. By using pumps Dye keeps the fresh water permanently two feet above the seawater level and since the fairways and the undulating greens are built at a minimum elevation of five feet above sea level there is three feet of dry sand to filter away water that does not reach the fairway drains.

Dye expected to recycle some 50,000 to 100,000 gallons of water a day through his drainage system but in fact recycles 300,000 gallons – 50 per cent of the water needed to irrigate the course and keep it green. He also pleased the locals by restoring a natural saltwater flow to 80 acres where the flow had been cut off by logging operations which had changed its character completely. What he has done at Kiawah, where no dirt was brought in to help with the construction, is a wonderful precedent for other water systems being installed in environmentally sensitive areas.

On British seaside links the grasses are bents and fescues. They can lie dormant and survive without much water in our climate and they produce that beautiful tight lie which is part of seaside golf. Because of the hot summers, bent grasses could not be used at Kiawah. Instead Bermudas, broader-leafed grasses that require constant watering, had to be planted thus ensuring that the course, while undeniably beside the seaside, could never be termed linkslike in character. In fact Dye used two Bermudas – a smaller-leafed variety for the approaches to the greens and the putting surfaces to allow players to bump-and-run shots up to the pin. In the dunes, in addition to the sea oats which spread so dramatically and had to be cut back before the match, he used American beach grass, panic grass, paspalum and the sweet grass that is weaved by Charleston craftsmen into baskets.

His aim was to bring back shotmaking under tournament con-

39

ditions. He claimed that since most American professional tournaments are played on courses where the requirement is for straight hitting to well-watered fairways and accurate iron play to greens that hold the ball, the art of shotmaking was being lost – a factor that Nicklaus has cited as a reason for recent European successes. Because we play on so many different types of course throughout the year on the Volvo Tour and in such varied conditions, the argument is that the average European Tour pro is, by necessity, a better shotmaker than his American counterpart.

From the tournament tees the Ocean course is 7315 yards long. Theoretically it can be stretched to a monster of 7756 yards by using the back tees – but that was never the designer's idea. It was purely to ensure the course, played from whatever tees were being used, would be a test in the winds which change direction so frequently there. Most holes have several tees affording as much as 100 yards leeway to allow for the wind, Dye's philosophy being that he did not want a great hole to become a nothing hole just because

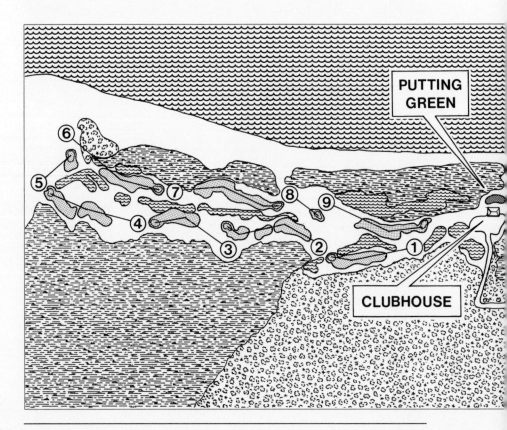

of a change in the wind direction. He did not want a hole that required a drive and 4-iron into the wind to become a 1-iron and wedge downwind. Chatting to him, he instanced the 13th, which he considered a superb test played at 350 or 470 yards with a green built in such an ingenious way that with the proper pin position it would suit a mid-iron or wedge equally well.

When I first visited Kiawah and had the chance to play with designer Dye and Dave Stockton, I was impressed. I liked the course. I could see what Dye had tried to do and thought that he had done it very well. I had read that Stockton had said that the course was ideal for European players because it was sure to be windy and it would require the playing of a lot of chip-and-run shots of the type that we are used to playing on Scottish and Irish seaside links. But the only things that I felt looked Scottish at Kiawah were the sand dunes, although there was a British seaside look to the view towards the clubhouse from the elevated tee at the short 14th.

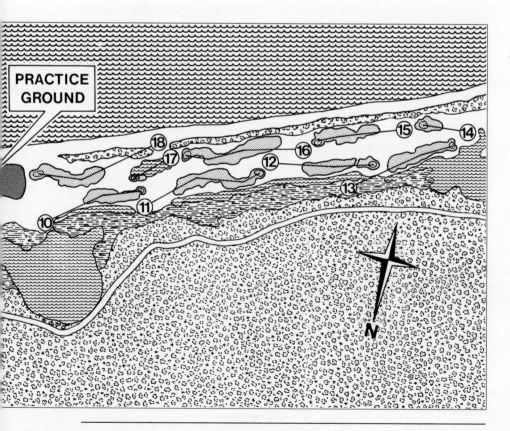

Dye gave you the impression that you were at a course in Europe but in between the dunes there was a distinct American style about the course, with one notable difference. There was no heavy collar of grass around the greens like those usually in place for a US Open or a USPGA Championship. This was quite deliberate. To have had collars around the greens would have forced players to hit high floaters into the pin which, in the potentially strong winds, could have made the course unfair. The greens were, in fact, very undulating and mostly banked up so that the chance of being able to throw the ball up and have it stop by the pin, like the Americans do in Tour events, was not always going to be possible. Dye had to give the players a way to get to the flag other than by the high lob.

I saw the course holding no great advantage to the European players who do not play many seaside courses during the season. I knew Stockton was well aware that American golfers play as much in the wind as we do, if not more, and that we do not play on that many seaside courses, but he was trying to gee up his side. He wanted to make the Americans feel that they were the underdogs in the hope that it would inspire them sufficiently to win back the Ryder Cup. His team was going to be ready. He was going to see to that.

Dave has not changed much since the days when we were on opposing Ryder Cup sides. He is a really nice fellow, but underneath there has always been a tough competitor and I was left in no two minds on my trip to Kiawah that he was desperate to lead his Cup team to victory. I mean desperate! He felt that he had been charged with the responsibility of getting the Cup back by the PGA of America, by the players who had taken so much flak about having lost it and failed twice to win it back, and by the golfing public.

The Ryder Cup had become a major sporting issue in the States and I got the distinct impression that he felt it was his duty to win it back for the American people. Stockton, I could see, was going to exceptional lengths as far as preparation was concerned. When he was not on the US Tour running the rule over likely players or speaking about the match at functions around the country, he was at Kiawah promoting the Cup and the controversial venue. Kiawah was far more remote than any other venue had been. There was plenty of accommodation available in nearby Charleston, one of the loveliest of cities in the southern United States, but little on the island and I knew our team, as a result, would not have the luxury of as big a following as they had had at Muirfield Village.

Although I admired the Ocean course, I must say I was disappointed that the PGA of America had gone to Kiawah rather than to one of the more established courses in the States of which there are so many. There were commercial considerations to take into account but Kiawah was not the best choice. When you look around America and see how many championship courses there are with superb hotel accommodation close by, you have to question the decision to choose a course for the match on an island with difficult access and limited facilities. Ideally I wanted a strong presence in the galleries for my side but as it turned out those that were there to support us did us proud. Still, on the first visit I couldn't see how 25,000 people would be able to see the play in comfort. The fairways were broad , however, and I knew it would be possible, at least, for the crowds to go along one side of them at some holes. The officials of the PGA of America were always confident there would be no trouble, although the spectators would be closer to the play than usual.

In fairness I have always felt that the American supporter does not follow matches and players as much as the British fan does. The American is far more likely to turn up at a golf event with a cooler of cold drinks and place himself all day in the one spot and let the players pass him. The problem at the Ryder Cup was that with only four foursomes and four fourballs a day for the first two days there was not going to be much action for the static spectator to watch and maybe none at all for the fan who decided to plant himself down by the green at the 18th. At one point Stockton half-suggested that we play five-game series for the first two days in order to give the static spectator more to see, but this was never raised officially and, anyway, since we held the Cup, we would have initiated any rules changes, not the Americans. In the Carolinas, I doubt whether we would have fitted in the foursomes and fourballs before dark – a factor later borne out on the second day of the match when Seve Ballesteros and Jose Maria Olazabal finished in near darkness against Payne Stewart and Fred Couples.

Dave did not mention it to me then but he did write subsequently

43

to the PGA in Britain to suggest that any European professional likely to be on our side would be made most welcome to travel to Kiawah to practise. He said his 'possibles' would be dropping in from time to time but I have to say I took the original offer to us as genuine enough on Dave's part but as a publicity stunt for Landmark. His team, chosen over two years, was nearly finalized. My team was not. I never suggested any of my players should go early. We had not gone early to Muirfield Village in 1987 to get to know that course, neither had the Americans come early to The Belfry in 1985 or 1989. I have always felt that any top-class player – and I knew I would have top-class players on my side – could fully familiarize himself with Kiawah in the three or four days between our arrival and the start of the match. In fact I do not believe many of his team went down to Kiawah anyway for serious practice in the early months of the year before the course was really ready, but that is all water under the bridge now.

On that first visit to the course I had been able to gather enough information to inform our players about the character of the course and the key holes on it, one of which undoubtedly was the short 17th. These days all course designers must, it seems, produce one classic hole, their signature hole. At Kiawah it had to be the 17th with its carry of 175 yards across one of the manmade irrigation lagoons. There was simply no let-out around the green. Even if you played left and tried to miss the water there was a bunker in an area of waste sand which could leave you with virtually no shot, as we were to discover. The green was two-tiered and hitting it with the wind blowing left to right as you stood on the tee would, I knew, be the pressure-shot in each match that got that far. It would test a player's character.

What really surprised me was that the 18th hole, by contrast, was remarkably straightforward and on the face of it quite easy. It did not strike me as being the sort of hole that would turn matches, which was quite different from the situation at Muirfield Village or at The Belfry where the 18th produced enough drama to satisfy even the most demanding fan. Yet I would be proved so wrong on that point! I had expected Dye to finish with something heroic by making the 18th a long testing par 4 with, say, a drive over water and a second shot over water instead of what it was – a drive and a

3- or 4-iron to a green certainly angled away from you but not difficult to hit downwind. The 18th would turn out, of course, to be much tougher than I had thought, helped by the fact that there was the pressure of the match to contend with and the wind was always against.

On my visit to Kiawah I also had a look at how the team might be accommodated. There was only one hotel on the island, the Kiawah Island Inn, but I knew that that would not be suitable. Catering might have been easier there but it would not have given the players the privacy I wanted them to have. The general atmosphere, in contrast to the formal evenings in my early Cup playing days, would be relaxed and I wanted to make sure that wherever the team was staying it would be exclusively for them, their families and no one else. We had found this to be important in previous years. It was after all a big week, a pressure-packed week. In the end I decided on apartments down by the sea. This meant that all our food would have to be brought in, but I did not see this as a problem. In fact, Lesley is a qualified dietician so one of her roles was going to be to supervise the daily menu, which can get complicated when you are catering for different nationalities. Seve Ballesteros, as always, tried to be helpful by even producing a list of the foods he felt would be acceptable to everyone. That did not mean that we would be having paella most nights!

In those vital early discussions I insisted we had three-room apartments for those players who might be bringing babies and a nanny, and especially for myself and Lesley because I wanted the team to eat there together every night. Team spirit had been a vital factor in our success from 1983. There had been a togetherness that had perhaps been lacking in the American side but which Stockton, I noted, was nurturing. By eating together it gave the members of the side the chance to discuss informally the problems of the course or of their games. It encouraged everyone to pull for everyone else. At the Ryder Cup golfers who are usually sporting rivals have to blend together as a unit helping and encouraging each other. When Dave Stockton heard of my request for an apartment big enough to have a team dining-room, he immediately followed suit.

Because the course was nine miles on to the island there was a

45

suggestion at one stage that the team might be taken to the first tee every morning along the beach, but this was ruled out when it was realized that it might be dangerous if the tide was in. We would instead be given our own cars and I did not envisage any real problems getting to the course during the match as our apartments were as near to it as possible. We were going to be accommodated well away from the general public, most of whom would be bussed in and out of Charleston. The only people on the island would be house owners and their guests, members of the official party and some of the leading press and television personnel, all of whom would be well away from us.

One other thing that Dave Stockton and I talked about was the procedure we might adopt regarding the availability of members of both sides to the press. We have come to the stage in the Ryder Cup where we know what we want and what works well and both of us were agreed that the teams would be introduced to the press on the Tuesday of match week and would be available then for comment. After that, only Dave and I would act as spokesmen at the official daily press conferences. That was the way the players wanted it. They were there to play golf that week and Dave and I both wanted them to be given the opportunity to do so without being hassled. However, neither of us objected to their being approached informally at the end of their practice rounds or games assuming they wanted to chat. It would be left to them.

Although the games and the Cup are always fiercely competitive it is a marvellous week for friendship and camaraderie. We all take it deadly seriously on the course during the match but before it begins and after it has been won and lost there is a tremendous spirit among the players of both sides. I heard David Feherty say when he made the team that he felt honoured to be joining a very exclusive but marvellously friendly club. It is, and I can understand why Feherty felt he was losing out on something until he had become a Cup team member.

Although I knew the agreement between the PGA and the Tour had not yet been signed, which remained a major worry, I was reasonably happy when I left Kiawah that everything was in order for the match. I knew, too, from Stockton's burning desire to win the match, that it would be as tough – maybe even tougher – than any

46

we had played since 1983. Stockton told me that he was not totally surprised to learn of his selection as captain, indeed it had been between him and Raymond Floyd for the 1989 captaincy. In addition to our obvious team spirit we had had continuity with Tony in charge for four matches. The Americans, changing captains each match, lacked this until Stockton chose Floyd as a wild card. Stockton was more proud of his appointment as captain than of anything else he had ever done in golf – even his two USPGA Championship wins. He cited his three goals as winning, having fun and creating good memories. His hope was that there would be goodwill on both sides and that all 24 players and their wives would take home a great experience that would be remembered for all their lives. His views and mine were remarkably similar. Both of us respected the history and tradition of the match, both of us were well aware of the very positive advantages it provided as far as sponsorship was concerned on both sides of the Atlantic. Now all we needed was a good close game, fairly and honestly contested, and he and I were determined that this would be the case.

47

4

Sensible Agreement

Back in Britain, the behind-the-scenes efforts to sort things out continued. The situation had become tense enough for Ken Schofield to call a special players' meeting at Sunningdale during the European Open to outline the facts and to ascertain their collective view of what should be done. The response was emphatic. Unless the proposed partnership agreement was signed by the start of the 1991 season, the PGA at The Belfry could not count on the Tour players supporting the match. The hardly surprising verdict by the players, which strengthened Ken Schofield's hand in the negotiations such as they were, spelled out a situation John Lindsey at PGA headquarters had not envisaged would occur. Now the future of the Ryder Cup *was* in danger. After months of wrangling, the Tour had had enough.

The Sunningdale meeting and decision gave a new impetus to the negotiations. Johnnie Walker, who sponsor the match on this side of the Atlantic and the European team for away games, were due to hold a press conference in their London headquarters, Landmark House, on Monday 5 November. The Tour and the PGA would be represented at the meeting and it would be an ideal time to announce that a settlement had been reached. My understanding was that both sides had finally agreed and that it was just a question of the PGA signing the document, but even at the eleventh hour there was a snag and by the Monday morning of the press conference the agreement had not been signed. When I heard this I suggested to Ken Schofield that it might be best if I did not go to the press conference but he persuaded me otherwise. I was sick of the whole stupid business.

Johnnie Walker duly announced their continued sponsorship of the Ryder Cup and PGA Cup matches as part of their overall sponsorship of golf but I knew they were uneasy at the continuing uncertainty about the partnership deal. Over the excellent buffet that Johnnie Walker's managing director Ian Ross had laid on for us, the reporters began chatting informally to John Lindsey, Ken Schofield and myself. We were in separate corners of the room holding mini-press conferences and I decided to act. I told my group of pressmen that if agreement was not reached quickly – very quickly – I would resign the captaincy. I knew that this would bring matters to a head and within a week one of the most unnecessary episodes in British golfing history had been resolved. The agreement was signed and a long sad saga in Ryder Cup history was over. Just what the PGA gained from their delaying tactics and brinkmanship I shall never know.

The statement announcing the Joint Venture Agreement was distributed on 21 November. The PGA had climbed down and the deal had no strings attached. The PGA's suggestion that any agreement should run for just 12 years and then be renegotiated had been unacceptable to the Tour. The deal that had been signed was for ever and it made allowance for any future disputes over venue. The Tour and the PGA would have the final choice in alternate years, starting in 1997. All the delay had cost the PGA was the original offer of a share in the profits from the Volvo PGA Championship on the Volvo Tour. Neil Coles, strong chairman of the PGA European Tour board of directors, said: 'The considerable time and effort that has gone into reaching this permanent agreement properly reflects the respect the Tour's members hold for the Ryder Cup and their desire to play a major role, on and off the course, in safeguarding the match.'

49

John Lindsey, the executive director of the PGA, said: 'We have safeguarded the PGA's involvement for ever more and both sides' lawyers are working towards a properly structured formal agreement. The 1993 match will be run in the same way but perhaps a limited company will have to be set up to run future matches in Europe.' Then, most significantly, he added: 'The major issues such as venue, television, money are all contractually agreed and I would hope there is no reason for us to disagree on any other matters.'

What the players were delighted about was that the Cup had been saved and when the 1991 Tour season got under way in Girona near Barcelona the golfers would be playing, not just for prize money, but for Ryder Cup points.

The news that the wrangle was over was headline material and filled several column yards in the newspapers. Now I knew the spotlight would next turn on the players as they battled for points throughout the summer of 1991. I anticipated that, as the season went on and the pressures to make the team increased, the significance of a contender's play would be highlighted by the press, further increasing the pressure on him if he was struggling a bit.

The Cup is big news these days and golf is attracting a far wider readership than it has ever done before. That inevitably means that more reporters on more newspapers, some which previously did not care too much for golf coverage, are looking for more head-line-making stories. To be honest, I have always been suspicious of the press. So many journalists are not really interested in covering the golf but are always looking for an angle; if there is not an obvious one, then one will mysteriously appear. I have been upset too many times by what has been written about me, especially in the earlier years! Remember I have been around since 1968. Some journalists have an unnecessarily harsh edge to their reports. I am the same as anyone else trying to make a living on Tour. We are all trying to win. We are all doing our best and trying to shoot low scores but sometimes newspaper stories can be very cruel. Maybe I am ultra-sensitive on this subject but that is the way I feel.

I am different from Tony Jacklin, my predecessor, who may not always have enjoyed dealing with the press in years gone by, but who revelled in the role of Cup and team spokesman when he was captain. The up-front role suited him. I do not particularly like it although I knew that it would be one of my responsibilities when I took on the job. To be truthful I deliberately played down the captaincy and was criticized for this in some of the tabloid press. I was particularly disappointed when it was suggested at one stage, close to match time, that I might not even be in charge of the side any more and that Seve had taken over. I would like to put paid to that rumour. Seve was a tremendous support but I remained totally in charge. Of course I made mistakes. I do not deny that and maybe did not care to see some of even the justified criticism in print. Yet sometimes the stories got out of hand.

During the time of the Open Championship at Royal Birkdale I had been asked to assess the Europeans for the *Sunday Mirror*. The newspapers had contracted me to do a series of pre-Ryder Cup match articles similar to those Tony had done in previous years. I said in a preview to the Championship that I felt that Jose Maria Olazabal was quite capable of winning the Open and gave my reasons why – simply that he was ready to win after his near success at the US Masters. Backing up my team members for Kiawah I further suggested that Ian Woosnam, cheered on by his pals from Oswestry, could go well; that the rejuvenated Seve was ready to win again; and that Nick Faldo, who always played well at Birkdale, could do what he had done in Augusta a year earlier – successfully defend. In fact I suggested that they would fill the top four spots at Royal Birkdale – and they were good enough to do so. If that happened it meant the best Payne Stewart, the US Open champion, and Fred Couples could do would be to finish joint fifth! I did not say that I thought an American was not good enough to win; I was just saying why four of the top European players bound for Kiawah might take the leading places.

51

What happened was that some sections of the press spoke with Peter Alliss between commentaries and contacted Bob Tway, the former USPGA champion, and asked both to comment on my alleged assertion that no American was good enough to win the Open or even finish in the frame. Tway said basically that if that was what I had said I was thick and that he could not wait for the Europeans to come to Kiawah so that United States players could show my men how to play. What I had done could serve, he said, to wind up the Americans even more. I knew they were determined to beat us and I am not daft enough to say anything that would get them even more wound up than they were. I was just as determined as Stockton that my team would win, but that did not mean turning it into a hate match. Alliss called my remarks, as he was told them, stupid. The headlines called me arrogant for thinking the way I had. It upset me so much that I decided to abandon my *Sunday Mirror* column, but later I resurrected it to give my side of the 'Who-is-in-charge?' controversy.

The captaincy was new to me and I was learning a lot about the job itself and the people with whom I was having to deal. As captain I was required to handle a whole range of topics but I realized how much I needed to be on my guard. When Tony had handed over to me he had told me to treat the press side of the job with considerable care. This I did in the weeks leading up to the match by keeping any comments I made to a minimum and steering away from any potential controversy.

I knew I would have to do dozens of television interviews so, in order to make myself more at home with the cameras, I had signed up the previous year with what was then British Satellite Broadcasting, later to become Sky Sports. This I felt would help me improve my television technique. I did pieces to camera and discussed the play in the studio when the overseas broadcasts were being beamed in live. Learning about television gave me an insight into what goes on behind the scenes as well as in front of camera. I found it fascinating, if time consuming, but I was determined that, come the day, I would be as fluent and as comfortable in front of the cameras as the American players always appear to be.

Throughout the summer of 1990 and 1991 I continued to run the club shop at Wentworth. I suppose every club would love to have their professional appointed captain of the Ryder Cup team and Wentworth and its members were no exception. The new owners were particularly kind, giving me time off to involve myself in Cup business, and Elliot Bernerd and his board afforded me all the help and cooperation I needed to do the Cup job in the proper manner. During the build-up to the Cup I made a few speeches but did not travel as extensively for Johnnie Walker in Europe as Tony Jacklin had done two years earlier. Whenever I did appear at a press conference I kept being asked one question: 'How do you feel following Tony Jacklin – surely the toughest of acts to follow?' Of course it was, but I always pointed out that neither Jacklin nor I would hit one ball in the Ryder Cup and that the players were the ones who did the work.

I often wondered how some of my predecessors had handled the million and one things that can and do go wrong. The men I had played under were all different . . . Eric Brown, a great motivator and noted American-basher! . . . Bernard Hunt, a gentleman . . . Brian Huggett, somewhat aloof . . . John Jacobs, the European Tour's staunchest supporter, who had been its guiding light in its formative years . . . and Jacklin. I always felt he had an advantage over the others in that he was around at a time when he still had a remarkable rapport with the players because of his age and repu-tation. Unlike any of the others, he did not have to work within a strict PGA budget. In the days of Brown, Hunt and Jacobs there was only a limited amount of money; first-class travel across the Atlantic was out of the question.

A big difference between the teams then and now was the way we were dressed for the match and the quality of the clothing pro-vided. This time Glenmuir equipped us for the course and Oscar Jacobsen and Boss provided the suits, jackets, trousers and so on. Because of our recent successes, suppliers are more than willing now to give us the best quality. That was not always the case. In the old days we took what we could get, unlike the Americans who had everything from the top drawer. It was easy to feel inferior when we looked across at the big money earners as they flashed their gold Rolex watches at us. We were not jealous of them, just envious of the arrangements made on their behalf. Now we flash our gold Rolex watches back at them.

Because the team is finalized only a few weeks before the match takes place it is not easy to get everyone fitted out, so we had an early-season session at the Volvo PGA Championship when I selected 20 possible Cup men and had them measured up. They knew that only 12 would be selected and one or two of them refused to be fitted out for superstitious reasons, but generally everyone cooperated. In due course every team member received two blaz-ers, two pairs of slacks, a suit, two pairs of dress shoes, four shirts, two ties and a suitcase to put them in. The on-course gear comprised two pairs of slacks for each of the six days of practice and play, two sports shirts for each day in a variety of colours, a long- and short-sleeved sweater, a rain suit, an umbrella, a golf bag, a holdall, two pairs of golf shoes and several pairs of socks. I even got to choose the styles and the colours and I plumped for safe plain colours on which the Ryder Cup logo could be spotted easily in close-up on NBC's 21 hours of mammoth TV coverage, the largest ever. In addition the caddies were fitted out with complementary coloured shirts and slacks.

It had been a tradition, started when Tony Jacklin took over, that the players travel with their regular caddies. Their travel and accommodation is paid but there is a curious anomaly in that at away matches the European caddies are paid by the PGA of America. That caused a problem. The Americans, who seemed remarkably naive in many aspects of the Cup arrangements, announced that they would give the caddies $500 for the week, which prompted an immediate response from a couple of our more senior men, arguing that this was totally inadequate. I had to agree with them. Kiawah was not an easy course to play and it was cer-tainly a difficult one for a caddie to work. Since the players do not get paid during Cup week the caddies were not in line for any bonus payments. Realizing the legitimacy of their claim, I convened a quick meeting with John Lindsey and Ken Schofield to sort out what I could see was a ridiculous situation. Although the players pay weekly wages to their caddies, I felt that during Ryder Cup week the caddies are under as much pressure as the players and that the sum suggested by the Americans needed to be topped up by us. I felt that we had a good sponsor in Johnnie Walker, that the Cup now does make money and that it was our responsibility, not the players', to look after this. It was agreed an extra $700 would be paid, giving them, in sterling, the equivalent of £600 for the week or £100 a day for what I knew were going to be six long, hard days of grafting.

The caddies are a tremendous group of fellows, highly profes-sional and well able to play their part in keeping the players calm and focused on the course. They stayed in villas arranged for them by the Americans and were given one car between three to make them totally independent. The only problem we found when we got there was providing them with an adequate breakfast! The PGA of America had made no arrangements for them, believing, I suppose, that, like the American caddies, they could go to the supermarket on the island, stock up their apartments and make their own breakfasts before they came to the course. The American caddies may have been used to doing this but our fellows were not. That was eventually sorted out but at least I knew they ate well in the evening, and deservedly so.

Preparations for the Ryder Cup continued throughout the summer and the match increasingly dominated my everyday life. I ran and reran in my mind all the scenarios I thought might occur during the week, assessing how I would handle them, remembering how Tony had dealt with this awkward issue or that. One of the problems I was not looking forward to handling was any disciplinary matter. Players had stepped out of line before, so badly in 1979 at The Greenbrier that John Jacobs, the captain that year, had been faced with the task of deciding whether or not to send the players home. I could not imagine finding myself in that situation at Kiawah, however, because of the way the team was shaping up.

Over in America the battle for Ryder Cup points and a place in their side had been running from 1 January 1990. Only in its closing stages did I become interested in who might or might not make the side.

Let me for a moment talk about the selection methods used on either side of the Atlantic. Since 1947 the American team has been chosen on a dedicated-points basis, sometimes over two years but, in the late 1970s and early 1980s, over one. After losing in 1985, the Americans – at the suggestion of Jack Nicklaus – reverted to a two-year system as Jack felt this would ensure that the best players made the team. The top 10 on their points table would be selected automatically and the captain would choose two more at his discretion. The requirement that the USPGA champion should be one of those wild cards if he failed to make the side automatically no longer applied for 1991 and cost John Daly a Cup place. Next time the Americans will again collect points over two seasons but the events played in 1993 will carry double points, thus reducing the chance of players who are out of form during Ryder Cup year making the side, as in the case of Wayne Levi in 1991.

55

The ways of choosing our side over the years have been many and varied according to Michael Williams, who wrote the excellent official history of the Cup. In 1983 the whole team was chosen from the money list on a £1 = 1 point basis but two years later, with the top Europeans playing more in America, some room for manoeuvre had to be allowed to ensure those players competing regularly in the States would have the chance to make the side. It was decided that nine would come off the points table, running from the first tournament of the year to the event which fell four weeks before the match, and that the captain would choose the final three players himself – and that is the system we use today.

There is sense in this. Although our top players have now given up their US Tour cards, they still compete 10 or 11 times in America so our three wild cards are essential. American players, however, tend to stick to their own Tour and they seem to be happy enough with their own system of two wild cards as they have retained it for the 1993 Cup. I see no reason for uniformity and felt Dave Stockton's call for similar systems was quite unnecessary.

At the start of the 1991 season, the Americans had been collecting points for almost 10 months and when Tom Kite came out and won the Tournament of Champions at Carlsbad, he moved into seventh spot. The list on 7 January 1990 – a full month before the Europeans even started collecting points – the US top 20 looked like this:

1.	Fred Couples	425	11.	Mark O'Meara	245
2.	Payne Stewart	391	12.	Chip Beck	232
3.	Wayne Levi	372	13.	Larry Mize	223
4.	Paul Azinger	348	14.	Loren Roberts	185
5.	Hale Irwin	340	15.	Peter Jacobsen	175
6.	Tim Simpson	326	16.	Mark Brooks	167
7.	Tom Kite	314		Corey Pavin	167
8.	Mark Calcavecchia	292	18.	Mike Donald	157
9.	Lanny Wadkins	287	19.	Jim Gallagher	153
10.	Gil Morgan	248	20.	Bob Tway	146

That list included nine of the eventual team in the top 12. The players not there at the end of the lengthy points-counting period were Tim Simpson, who missed out narrowly, Tom Kite and Dr Gil Morgan. By the end of our Open at Birkdale, a championship which had the distinction of counting for both US and European

Ryder Cup points, the American table showed very little change except that Corey Pavin, by now No. 1 in the money list helped by victories in the Bob Hope Desert Classic and the Bell South Atlanta Classic, had forced his way up from tied 16th to sixth in the table; Mark O'Meara had moved up from 11th to seventh; and Tom Kite and Gil Morgan had slipped out of the 'automatic' list. Steve Pate, who had won the Honda Classic earlier in the year, had become a team candidate in 12th spot and Chip Beck was lying 14th. Pate would force himself in ahead of Simpson at the USPGA Championship but Kite could produce nothing that would have continued his distinguished Cup career and off-form Curtis Strange and, more surprisingly, Tom Watson were not even in the top 20.

When the USPGA Championship at Crooked Stick was over the final standings were:

1.	Fred Couples	721	11.	Tim Simpson	392
2.	Payne Stewart	546	12.	Tom Kite	357
3.	Lanny Wadkins	525	13.	Chip Beck	339
4.	Hale Irwin	517	14.	Gil Morgan	314
5.	Paul Azinger	501	15.	Scott Hoch	313
6.	Corey Pavin	498	16.	Jim Gallagher Jnr	300
7.	Mark O'Meara	425	17.	Bruce Lietzke	297
8.	Mark Calcavecchia	407	18.	Davis Love III	291
	Wayne Levi	407	19.	Mark Brooks	290
10.	Steve Pate	405	20.	Bob Tway	267

57

Ten of the American team had been finalized and Stockton wanted another day to consider whom he might add to make up the side. In the automatic 10 there were three newcomers – Corey Pavin, Steve Pate and Wayne Levi, who had stayed in the top 10 despite his poorer 1991 form. Stockton then leap-frogged Tim Simpson and Tom Kite to opt for Chip Beck, who was by now in 13th position in the table, and plumped, too, for the experience of Raymond Floyd, who was in 23rd spot in the final table. This was a decision that I am sure disappointed Jack Nicklaus who had indicated he was available, devastated Kite and came as a body blow to Simpson and Tom Watson, the other candidates. As far as Nicklaus was concerned there was no question that he had been passed over because the American players did not want him in the team. There was a time when having Jack Nicklaus in the US side scared our players. In 1991, selecting Nicklaus would have scared the *American* team more than us. The Americans would have been more intimidated by Jack's presence than our fellows would have been.

I thought at the time that Stockton's selections were curious but, as it would turn out, there was nothing wrong with them. Clearly he had chosen Beck because he had teamed up well with Azinger at The Belfry two years earlier and Floyd because he saw him as an ideal partner for Fred Couples. They had scored a brilliant success as a partnership in the Greg Norman-hosted RMCC Invitational in which they played better ball in the first round (a form of foursomes with both players hitting the tee shots then deciding which ball to use) and a scramble. They had fired 64, 57 and 61 – a three-day total of 34 under par. Raymond was clearly a good influence on Couples on that occasion and would be again at Kiawah. Dave Stockton had always laid great store on team spirit and in getting together a side that would pair up well in foursomes and fourballs. Strong partnerships were the key, he felt, to getting back the Cup.

Looking at their side, chosen two weeks before ours, I felt that although my team was not finalized I would be going to America with players who could win, providing the Spaniards Seve Ballesteros and Jose Maria Olazabal, along with Ian, Nick and Bernhard – our top five – played to their usual form. I thought that Payne Stewart would turn out to be their strongest player; that Fred Couples, even with Floyd by his side, could buckle under pressure (although I would be proved very wrong); that Floyd at 49 might, in fact, be too old for three days of tough competition on a hard-to-walk course; and that Mark Calcavecchia was very inconsistent. Wayne Levi was a definite weak link, having shown no form during the year, and Paul Azinger, I felt, might not produce his best form because of all the injuries, especially the shoulder problem, he had suffered during the season and which had caused him to miss the Open and the USPGA Championships. Corey Pavin and Steve Pate were unknown quantities to me although Pavin did for a time play in Europe and I knew that he was a hot putter. So saying I considered him a less impressive No. 1 on the US money list than many others in the past. Chip Beck and Mark O'Meara I considered consistent without being outstanding and Lanny Wadkins, although having a wonderful Cup record and being an 'as-hard-as-nails' competitor who could play with anyone, might be playing one Cup match too many . . . and that went, too, for Hale Irwin.

It was likely that any player in the European side would be able to handle anyone on the American team but I kept my views private. Whatever the composition of my team, I would be telling them that we would have a very tough battle on our hands. To have said otherwise might have allowed a measure of complacency to creep in. What is so very encouraging to me is that European golf has come on so well that today we can travel to America knowing we will give as good as we get and that the Americans expect a close, tough match. Up to 1983, and even in that year, we never went to America believing we could win.

So, the American team, chosen over almost two years, had been announced but here in Europe the players had two more events to play before our team was finalized. The Cup and the battle for places in the team had dominated the season but the final two weeks of points collecting would turn out to be far more tense than I ever imagined it could be.

59

· 5 ·

Down to the Wire

Originally there were to have been 28 points-counting events before the Cup team was finalized, but lack of finance put paid to the El Bosque Open, and the Gulf War scuttled the Dubai Desert Classic early in the season. Traditionally, some players find their form as the season goes on while others are on form when it begins and that certainly was the case with tall, broad-shouldered Steven Richardson, son of a professional, a former English amateur champion and in his second year on Tour. Richardson, who had impressed me the year before when he was runner-up to Russell Claydon for the Sir Henry Cotton Rookie of the Year prize, had no thoughts of making the Ryder Cup team when he began his season. He just wanted to continue improving and by that he meant winning a Volvo Tour event in 1991. He did much better: he won two of the first five, came second in another and fourth in one of the other two. It wasn't a fast start, it was a whirlwind of an opening to the season and it saw him straight into Ryder Cup contention. His first victory came in the Girona Open near Barcelona in the first week of the year and then he battled through the wind to win the Portuguese Open on the Estela course on the Atlantic coast at

Povoa, north of Oporto. By the time he had teed up in the Benson & Hedges at St Mellion and finished joint fifth there, Richardson had amassed £152,274 in prize money or the equivalent in Ryder Cup points. That was 80 per cent of what I believed it would take to make the team.

Had it not been for Richardson, everyone would have been talking about the way Jose Maria Olazabal had begun his year, the year he planned to win a major and the year I thought he would. He won the Catalan Open, a tournament he and his manager, Sergio Gomez, had organized on a new Robert Trent Jones course which had some marvellous holes and some marvellously fiendish ones too. He also finished third twice, 11th and 19th in the early season run through Europe and was poised to break through the 100,000 points mark by the end of the Benson & Hedges, eight weeks into the season.

Much to my satisfaction Bernhard Langer, Ian Woosnam and Sam Torrance had all won early season events in Europe and to add to my delight Ian had scored his first victory in America at New Orleans where he beat Jim Hallet in a play-off and went on to take the Green Jacket at Augusta where he pipped Olazabal. That had been a brilliant performance before fans mostly supportive of Tom Watson who finished third. Although the points table two months into the season was looking reasonably good, it was lacking the names of Nick Faldo and Seve Ballesteros. Seve had played only two of the first eight events and finished 33rd in Majorca thanks to a best of the day last round. He had missed the cut in the Catalan event, won by Olazabal, a bitter pill to swallow considering their close rivalry. Indeed it is a combination of their rivalry, their desire to outdo each other, allied to their tremendous respect for each other that has made them one of the greatest Ryder Cup partnerships in history, if not the ultimate.

Faldo's absence was easily explained. He concentrates his schedule on building up to the majors and after failing narrowly to win an unprecedented third Masters in a row, it was only then that he was ready to make his European debut at the Benson & Hedges. He finished the tournament, played in bitter cold and wind and won by Langer, well down the field. With Nick, one of the most dedicated golfers, I knew there was unlikely to be a problem. I antic-

61

ipated he would turn on the style for the big occasions that were to come and was firmly of the view, at that time, that he might even retain his Open title, especially since the Championship was being played at Royal Birkdale, a course he liked and over which he had won. After the Benson & Hedges the top 12 on the table read like this, with the winners on the Volvo Tour in capital letters:

1.	Steven RICHARDSON	152,247
2.	Jose Maria OLAZABAL	99,557
3.	Michael McLean	77,299
4.	Bernhard LANGER	66,660
	Ian WOOSNAM	66,660
6.	Sam TORRANCE	57,682
7.	Miguel Angel Jiminez	54,240
8.	Anders Forsbrand	47,694
9.	Miguel Angel Martin	46,302
10.	David Feherty	45,320
11.	Jose Rivero	44,502
12.	Barry Lane	37,733

Michael McLean's high rating had been helped by his second-place finish to Woosnam in the Fujitsu Mediterranean Open, which he had appeared to have won with a few holes to play, and his third-place finish in the Catalonian event. Torrance, with his extended putter, the one he tucks under his chin, had won in the wind at Jersey, an important point to note considering the chances of our playing the Cup match later in the year in a perpetual and ever swirling breeze.

Throughout the early weeks of points collecting I kept my own council, but later I discussed matters from time to time with Seve, Nick, Ian and Bernhard, the most experienced players whom I expected would make the side automatically anyway. I told them how I felt about the captaincy and that I wanted to leave alone those golfers who were trying to make the team. It was important in my mind that they get on with the business of making a living in the early part of the year. Certainly I did not intend to add to the pressures by constantly contacting them or talking to them about the Cup, or even by playing with the possibles on my own tournament appearances. I wanted to play it all down and reduce the hype, in contrast to Dave Stockton in America. For him the Ryder Cup lasted the whole year, culminating at Kiawah. For me it was just one important week in a busy year.

By 13 May, the 11th week into the season, Richardson was still No. 1, but Cup hopeful David Feherty from Northern Ireland, who had won the Cannes Open at Mougins, had eased himself into second place ahead of Olazabal who had taken two weeks off after narrowly losing the US Masters to Woosnam. McLean, Langer, Miguel Angel Martin, Torrance, Woosnam and Andrew Sherborne, who had held off the challenge of Mark James and Martin to win his first Tour event, the Madrid Open at Puerto de Hierro, filled the first nine spots following the Peugeot Spanish Open. But what excited me most of all that 11th week into the season was Seve's return to form. I had been worried about him at the start of the year but he had gone off to Japan two weeks earlier to play in two events and had taken the chance to discuss his putting and game generally with Nick Faldo's coach, David Leadbetter. Seve had used a Ping Putter for 15 years but changed to a Tad Moore and, for the first time since winning the Majorcan Open in March 1990 in a play-off with Magnus Persson, he took first prize in the Chunichi Crowns.

When Seve returned to Europe he was charged up and eager for another success. This was just what I wanted and I hoped that it was not a temporary burst of enthusiasm. I knew our chances of retaining the Cup at Kiawah depended on Seve not just being there but playing well and being at his inspirational best. I had seen what he could do to the morale of the team in previous years with his fierce commitment to European victory. The key upward move in the table came from Ballesteros when, on his return from the Far East, he should have beaten Eduardo Romero from the Argentine for the Spanish title. He lost to him in a seven-hole play-off which finished in near darkness at Club de Campo, the course that Seve and the Spaniards had touted months earlier as a possible Cup venue. By finishing second he leapt from 117th in the Johnnie Walker points table to 14th. On 13 May, after the Peugeot Spanish Open, the table read like this:

63

1.	Steven RICHARDSON	180,274
2.	David FEHERTY	114,368
3.	Jose Maria OLAZABAL	102,497
4.	Michael McLean	86,629
5.	Bernhard LANGER	82,825
6.	Miguel Angel Martin	78,967
7.	Sam TORRANCE	69,404
8.	Ian WOOSNAM	66,660
9.	Andrew SHERBORNE	59,739
10.	Miguel Angel Jiminez	52,400
11.	Anders Forsbrand	51,964
12.	Jose Rivero	47,100

When the vote had gone against Spain for the 1993 Cup venue, Seve had said in the press tent that the Ryder Cup match, which he had so firmly supported, would no longer mean quite so much to him, which for me, as captain, was worrying to hear. Later, of course, he would change his mind. By the end of May he was back to something like his best and hit a 5-iron to three feet for a birdie at the first extra hole at Wentworth to win the Volvo PGA Championship after a spirited duel with Colin Montgomerie, another golfer I always anticipated would make the side. He then went to Woburn and won the Dunhill British Masters for a second time, and I knew he was back and enjoying his golf again. When he won the Dunhill he was scoring his 63rd success around the world and it was his 47th win in Europe – two statistics which emphasized the great influence he has been on European golf since he started winning back in 1976.

By now Ireland's Eamonn Darcy was beginning to make his presence felt. He had finished fifth in the Cannes Open but had been soaked there, causing a recurrence of a back problem. After a three-week break he was back to finish third in the Volvo PGA Championship and then came second in the Dunhill to Seve. He was second again, this time after a play-off to Tony Johnstone in the Murphy's Cup. How significant that would turn out to be, although neither of us knew it at the time. I had noted he had said to the press that he was not interested in playing in the Ryder Cup again if he did not finish in the top nine and earn his place automatically, but I suspected the big Irishman really wanted to play. Still, true to my policy of not chatting about the match to any of them early in the season before their places were secured, I decided to say nothing. I had no idea then that it would all work out so badly for Eamonn. Every two years there is someone who loses out and in 1991 it would be Eamonn Darcy who would draw the short straw and suffer the biggest disappointment, but that was still to come. In early June he was likely, I felt, to be on the team and by 10 June he had moved into third place on the table.

Richardson and Seve, who were at the top of the table, had secured their team places. So a most talented newcomer and our most experienced and successful European, who thrives on match-play and performs with the same flair and dramatic excitement as a bullfighter does in a Spanish ring, were the first two to sign on for Kiawah. Seve's adversary is normally the course but in the Ryder Cup he has flesh and blood to battle against too. Far more exciting! I recalled when he and Paul Azinger had met in the singles at The Belfry in 1989, they had given each other nothing; no putts, not even the short ones. It was not that they disliked each other but rather that the intensity of the Cup match is such that it forces a player into being at his most patriotically competitive. They had respect for each other but by the same token refused to give each other one inch. It would be more difficult now in the Cup to concede a putt of the length that Jack Nicklaus did in 1969 to Tony Jacklin. Of course we would all like to think that we would do so in similar circumstances, but if it meant the possibility of earning another point for Europe we would all have to think long and hard about it. Jack's sporting gesture 22 years ago ensured that the underdog British and Irish side did not suffer its usual defeat. Today with the American backs to the wall, I reckon they would need to see everything within reason holed if they wanted to avoid a post-mortem afterwards.

I know how much it means to players on either side of the Atlantic to make the team, but I did not contact Steven Richardson until he had topped the 190,000 points mark. I knew then he was a certainty. I explained to him that far from ignoring him I had been monitoring his performance carefully and he understood that fully. I was sure, I told him, that he would be a major success in the team. Curiously by 10 June, 15 weeks into the 26 weeks points-counting period, eight of the then top nine would go on to make the side.

65

After the Murphy's Cup competition at Fulford the list looked like this, and only Darcy and Montgomerie, of the top nine, had not won:

1.	Seve BALLESTEROS	199,217
2.	Steven RICHARDSON	191,354
3.	Eamonn Darcy	130,087
4.	Ian WOOSNAM	126,088
5.	David FEHERTY	124,665
6.	Sam TORRANCE	116,088
7.	Jose Maria OLAZABAL	112,046
8.	Bernhard LANGER	107,825
9.	Colin Montgomerie	100,190
10.	Michael McLean	87,999
11.	Miguel Angel Martin	83,682
12.	Costantino Rocca	70,884

A fortnight later Nick Faldo won, keeping a promise he had made to himself at the US Open at Hazeltine that he would win before he turned up at Royal Birkdale to defend his Open title in July. He won the Carrolls Irish Open at Killarney. It was a victory which did as much to boost him psychologically as it did to heighten my hopes that he would, after all, make the automatic top nine. Yet a month later he had still not made it. His Cup partner Woosnam had won again, this time in Monte Carlo, to clinch his Cup spot; Olazabal and Torrance had tied second in the French Open behind Argentinian Eduardo Romero; and Montgomerie was going along nicely having chased Faldo home in Ireland to take second place there. The names in the top nine on 7 July were the same as they had been on 10 June, only the order was shuffled, and Faldo had moved up into 11th spot with the Open still to come. In the Belgian Open Per-Ulrik Johansson had won in a play-off against Paul Broadhurst, but apart from noting how well both these players were doing – and also that Spain's Jose Rivero, Scotland's Gordon Brand Jnr and England's Mark James, all Cup men of experience, were well placed to make a move from 17th, 18th and 19th spots in the table respectively – I remained relaxed and open-minded. There would be time to think about pairings nearer the time, after the Open Championship or maybe even later after the string of big-money events that followed the Birkdale championship. So much could happen with our £1 = 1 point system that I was prepared just to let things roll along. I anticipated that the way the table looked before the Open would be very different from the way it would look after the Dutch Open and the Scandinavian Masters in the succeeding weeks as the three events accounted for 2 million points. On 17 July, the eve of the Open, the table read like this:

1.	Seve BALLESTEROS	206,416
2.	Steven RICHARDSON	201,158
3.	Ian WOOSNAM	193,016
4.	Jose Maria OLAZABAL	160,933
5.	Colin MONTGOMERIE	153,265
6.	Sam TORRANCE	150,748
7.	David FEHERTY	137,212
8.	Eamonn Darcy	130,087
9.	Bernhard LANGER	115,384
10.	Anders Forsbrand	110,925
11.	Nick FALDO	102,310
12.	Michael McLean	94,208

Martin, Costantino Rocca from Italy, Johansson, Mats Lanner who was still going well, Rivero, Brand Jnr, James and David Gilford made up the 20. Paul Broadhurst at this stage was lying 25th. He had not yet come sharply into focus. What I was looking for now was a good performance from Nick Faldo in the £998,000 Open Championship so that he could clinch his place automatically. I was looking, too, for Brand Jnr and James to give themselves a leg up the table with useful cheques, although Gordon, I had been noting, seemed unable to switch himself into top gear, no matter how hard he tried, and Mark was waiting ever so patiently for something to happen and nothing was. I hoped Olazabal, too, would have a good Open; indeed I still fancied that he might win it. From the purely selfish standpoint of the Ryder Cup captaincy, however, I wanted all my key players to be in the side by the end of the Open or at worst by the end of the £600,000 Scandinavian Masters.

While Nick did not retain his title at Royal Birkdale, Eamonn Darcy, playing as well as he has ever done, finished as the top European, tied fifth behind the Australian winner Ian Baker-Finch. It was clear now that Nick would not manage to make it automatically because he was not playing any more points-counting events before the cut-off time at the end of the German Open in late August. He would get one of the wild cards and I announced that

67

ahead of schedule to avoid any speculation about his participation. He was one of my key men and there would have been an outcry had I left out the double Open and double Masters champion.

Bernhard Langer, determined to make the automatic top nine, did so with a second-place finish behind Payne Stewart, the US Open champion, in the Dutch Open at Noordwijk the week after the British Open, and it was in that event that Per-Ulrik Johansson had a 62 in the third round, to remind me that he wanted to make the side in his rookie year. Then Colin Montgomerie achieved what he had been striving to do all season – he won the Scandinavian Masters, edging out among others Woosnam and Ballesteros. By moving into second place in the Cup table he became my second Cup rookie. The Swedish event produced a third first-time cap in David Feherty, sixth in Holland and fifth in Sweden. I was delighted for him because he had been disappointed on two previous occasions. By 4 August I was beginning to take a much more careful note of what was happening. Six players plus Faldo were now 'in', but the battle was only beginning for the remaining spots. With just three more points-counting tournaments to go, the table read like this:

1.	Seve BALLESTEROS	307,734
2.	Colin MONTGOMERIE	275,015
3.	Ian WOOSNAM	246,851
4.	Steven RICHARDSON	240,048
5.	Bernhard LANGER	186,528
6.	David FEHERTY	184,375
7.	Eamonn Darcy	175,623
8.	Jose Maria OLAZABAL	174,533
9.	Sam TORRANCE	159,868
10.	Per-Ulrik Johansson	133,163
11.	Nick FALDO	119,865
12.	Anders Forsbrand	119,555

At this stage there was still a chance that one of the two Swedes would make it. Gilford was lying 16th and Broadhurst 22nd, but Paul jumped up 11 places when he won the European Pro-Celebrity at Hoylake with a final round of 66 that included nine birdies in 11 holes. When the season began I had felt that the likely qualifying total would be 180,000 points; now I thought it would be closer to 190,000. I did not ask for any special pairings in tournaments until the English Open came along at The Belfry, when I asked Ken Schofield whether there was a chance of Johansson playing with Seve. Although still outside the top nine, I wanted to see how he would react under pressure at a time when he was trying to get into the team. I suppose I wanted further evidence that he was ready for Cup competition. Maybe it was a bit unfair on Per-Ulrik but he came through the test with flying colours. As part of my earlier decision to keep the top players informed about things, my wife and I had dinner with Seve and his wife at The Belfry to discuss tactics. It was during this meal that he reported how impressed he had been by the way Per-Ulrik had played and handled himself. The Swede did enough at the English Open to convince me that if I had the opportunity to choose him I could do so with confidence. He was young, and I wanted young players in the side, and I thought he would be the first Swede to play in the Ryder Cup, but the circumstances just did not work out well for him and he did not make it.

That week at The Belfry I played with two more Cup hopefuls; Rocca from Italy and Gilford, who would go on to win the title despite being pressured by Ballesteros on the final day. Contrary to popular opinion, this was a draw I had not asked for. It just happened that way. On the 1st tee I explained to both of them that they should not read anything into the fact that they were playing with me, although I suspect a shrewd tournament director had spotted that it might be advantageous for me to be with them. I asked them just to play their own games and forget, if they could, that I was there. I pointed out that neither of them would be chosen as wild cards on two rounds at The Belfry. As it was they both played well. Gilford's win meant he edged out Olazabal from eighth spot and pushed Torrance down to 10th, outside the magic automatic nine.

The situation was becoming, in press terms, really interesting and for me, the man who would have to choose at the end of the German Open whom to add to the top nine, it was getting much more complicated. Faldo had won my support for one wild card and I knew Olazabal, who had won in America during the week of the English Open, would need one, too, if he dropped out of the top nine. Olazabal had taken The International title at Denver in Colorado, a victory which in many respects renewed his interest in

69

the game after the disappointment of having lost the Masters, a disappointment which had hung over him like a black cloud for several months. Yet I knew that so much could still happen. So many players were still in the running that absolutely nothing was certain. With just one points-counting event to go the table read like this:

1.	Seve BALLESTEROS	333,069
2.	Colin MONTGOMERIE	275,015
3.	Steven RICHARDSON	265,383
4.	Ian WOOSNAM	246,851
5.	Bernhard LANGER	186,528
6.	David FEHERTY	184,375
7.	Eamonn Darcy	182,145
8.	David GILFORD	177,883
9.	Jose Maria OLAZABAL	174,533
10.	Sam TORRANCE	164,188
11.	Per-Ulrik Johansson	150,567
12.	Paul BROADHURST	127,328
13.	Anders Forsbrand	121,230
14.	Nick FALDO	119,865
15.	Michael McLean	118,416
16.	Jose Rivero	105,061
17.	Miguel Angel Martin	104,264
18.	Costantino Rocca	102,834
19.	Peter Mitchell	100,674
20.	Mats Lanner	94,836
21.	Gordon Brand Jnr	90,666
22.	Mark James	90,308

70

Missing the cut in Holland and in Scandinavia, where he pulled a muscle in his shoulder, had suddenly put Torrance into the danger zone, although he was always on my wild-card list. Amazingly, because of the £500,000 prize fund in the Volvo German Open at Hubbelrath in Dusseldorf, 14 players were still capable of earning enough money to make the side automatically, although I knew most would have to win the title to do so. I knew that my wild-card options might be restricted somewhat by having to give a further wild card to Jose Maria.

Throughout the season I had played from time to time, just to keep my eye on what was happening and, quite simply, because I enjoy playing. I entered the German Open and flew to Dusseldorf on the Tuesday with an open mind on the Cup situation. Surprisingly I managed to get myself on the leader board for a time which prompted the usual comments in the press room that I was showing the lads the way. It was all tongue in cheek of course. By the final round I was off the leader board and certain Ryder Cup matters had been cleared up.

I had said that I would consider Ronan Rafferty and Sandy Lyle if either of them won. These two are very experienced and, although neither had had a good season, there were signs, I thought, that they were both running into form. I had never suggested that they would be chosen if they won in Germany, just that they would be put on my shortlist. You can imagine my surprise when I received some unexpected criticism about this from Ronan after he had completed his third round. He told the journalists that he felt it would be a disgrace if he or Sandy Lyle were chosen on one week's performance, but his comments indicated to me that he had not understood what I meant.

The Johnnie Walker points table going into the final round showed me that Seve Ballesteros, Steven Richardson, Colin Montgomerie, Ian Woosnam, Bernhard Langer and David Feherty were 'in'. There were three places to be played for and, of course, I still had my two wild cards. It was all desperately tight with Sam Torrance on top of the leader board after 54 holes. The situation with one round to go before the team was finalized was still fluid:

1.	Sam Torrance	69	67	69	205
2.	Gordon Brand Jnr	70	70	66	206
3.	Ronan Rafferty	70	70	67	207
	Mark McNulty	68	67	72	207
5.	Paul Broadhurst	73	67	68	208
	Rodger Davis	70	69	69	208
	Quentin Dabson	69	68	71	208
8.	Vijay Singh	67	71	71	209
	Jose Rivero	72	67	70	209
	Mark Roe	69	72	68	209
11.	Rick Hartmann	70	67	73	210
	Colin Montgomerie	70	71	69	210
	Chris Williams	66	70	74	210
	Mark James	70	73	67	210
	Sandy Lyle	67	69	74	210
	Barry Lane	71	66	73	210
	Philip Walton	71	72	67	210
18.	Peter Teravainen	72	70	69	211
	Christian Hardin	71	72	68	211
	Jeff Hawkes	70	69	72	211

(cont)	18.	James Spence	72	70	69	211
		John Bland	72	68	71	211
		David Gilford	69	73	69	211
		David J. Russell	72	70	69	211
		Daniel Silva	72	72	67	211
		Ross Drummond	70	70	71	211
		Peter Fowler	72	70	69	211
		Brian Barnes	71	72	69	211

I knew that for Eamonn to drop out of the top nine, three things had to happen: Sam Torrance had to finish in the top five, winning no less than the equivalent of fifth-place money; Paul Broadhurst had to finish in the top two, aware that a tied second-place cheque would not be enough to make him one of the automatic nine; and David Gilford had to win the equivalent of 34th-place money. The chances of all three of those things happening was, I felt, remote, but I was surprised that Eamonn had not come to Germany to make absolutely sure of his place. If I had known that he was not going to enter, I would have alerted him that he might want to reconsider because I could not give him any guarantee that he would be chosen if he did drop out of the top nine. I just assumed that he would turn up. He had been one of our heroes at Muirfield Village and, although he had said earlier in the season that he did not want to be selected to play, he had had such a good Open at Birkdale and seemed so certain to finish in the top nine that he had changed his mind and now wanted desperately to go to Kiawah. I knew he believed that he had much to offer the team, and his remarkable wedge play, on a course where I anticipated many greens would be missed, could be valuable.

I had been so sure that Eamonn would make the team that with just a few weeks of points collecting to go I had been discussing with him my wild-card options, canvassing his opinion as a potential team member. It never struck him, nor did it me, that with more than 182,000 points he would not be an automatic choice. As he sat at home that week and heard how things were developing on that final day in Germany, I knew that he would be desperately disappointed if he did not make the side automatically, but that he would probably still hope, maybe even expect, to get the final wild card if the unbelievable happened.

I had failed to maintain my early tournament form and when I finished my fourth round it was early enough to go for some lunch. I tried to keep out of the way as much as possible as I wanted to keep a clear mind for what I knew was going to be a difficult afternoon. I knew that Mark James had the support of the other senior team members as a wild-card choice, but it would be difficult to put him in and leave Torrance out if Sam slipped back in the final round and failed to make the top nine. I had heard that one of the popular daily papers in Scotland had suggested I had already given Sam a guaranteed spot, but I had not. Apart from Nick Faldo, no one else had been given any guarantees. Only Olazabal of the others could have considered himself sure of a place.

After a quiet lunch I went out on to the course to check out the candidates as inconspicuously as I could. Torrance was still doing all right. Paul Broadhurst, needing to finish second, was not exactly burning the course up but neither was he losing much ground. Gilford was dropping back a bit. He had been on no one's shortlist at the start of year but had proved his steely competitiveness under pressure at The Belfry. As the tournament continued it was clear that neither Lyle nor Rafferty were going to win, so it was with a certain sadness that I saw their chance of selection disappear. Johansson, whom I thought might make it, was also slipping out of contention on this sunny day at hilly Hubbelrath, but, on the other hand, Brand Jnr was still going well, and still had a chance of winning with nine holes to play. Twice before he had squeezed into the side with good performances late in the season but even if he won he knew now he would need to be selected. It might, I thought, come down to him or Mark or Sam, who was favourite in that scenario. As play continued there was no real pattern. No one was running away with it.

In mid-afternoon the leader board changed dramatically when someone not in the running for the Ryder Cup team, Mark McNulty, the Zimbabwean golfer who was defending the title, holed his second shot at the 12th. There had been those people who had suggested that our points-scoring system was unfair in that it was affected by players who were not in the running for the team. They argued that a system rewarding only the Europeans who were playing would be more satisfactory. I did not agree with that view, believing that overseas players on our leader boards actu-

73

ally forced our own players into producing even better performances. As I watched the leader boards I was aware that Brand Jnr was beginning to drop shots as the pressure on him intensified. The magic that had earned him a team place twice was not repeating itself but Broadhurst was not out of it, not by a long way. He had started the final round in 12th spot on the Cup table but to squeeze into the top nine his task, relative to those of Torrance and Gilford, was the most difficult. He had to move up from joint fifth place into second on his own.

The first of the trio to finish would be Gilford. Just as it looked as if his hopes of adding Ryder Cup honours to his Walker Cup appearance in 1985 were slipping, he had made three birdies in a row after the turn. Playing the last he was on the borderline. Two putts would definitely take him past Darcy, but in trying to make sure of his Cup place he raced his first putt 15 feet past the hole and then missed the return. Whether he made the team or not now depended on how many finished with him on his total. That meant another 45 minutes of agony in Dusseldorf for him and for Darcy in Dublin until the matter was clarified. Helped by Philip Walton taking 7 at the last, Gilford's group would end up joint 30th and, in that position, he would make just enough to move ahead of Darcy in the table.

As the afternoon wore on it still looked as if Eamonn would remain in the top nine and Sam would move back into it at Olazabal's expense and that my choices would be easy: Olazabal, who would have slipped to 10th, and Mark James. But Broadhurst had totally different ideas. He birdied the 17th and then rolled in a 20-footer for a birdie at the tough last hole in a late thrust that suddenly changed the situation completely. His birdie, birdie finish meant that he might do even better than second; he might win, because he was now tied with McNulty at the top of the leader board. Then, just adding to the complexity of the situation, Torrance, in a bunker off the tee, tumbled to a 7 at the 17th. The significance of this was that with Broadhurst in, on two under par, and Sam now unable to finish two under, Broadhurst could finish no worse than second on his own, just what he needed to do to pass Darcy. He had achieved his target. He had leap-frogged Eamonn and had, dramatically, made the team. I now had five rookies – Steven Richardson, Colin

Montgomerie, David Feherty, Paul Broadhurst and David Gilford – with guaranteed spots.

When you have taken a 7 you are a little bit apprehensive on the next tee, especially if it is the last tee and it is your one chance to make par to be sure of joining the Cup side automatically. That was the situation Sam found himself in as the battle for points, which had started seven months earlier in Spain, drew to its dramatic climax. If he failed to par and fell to 10th place in the points table, he would have to rely on my giving him a wild card and that would prevent my choosing Mark James. But there was even more significance to the last-hole performance of Torrance. Eamonn Darcy was still sweating it out in Ireland. For him the worst scenario had happened. He had slipped to eighth when Gilford passed him and ninth when Broadhurst finished second. If he was going to make the side automatically he needed Sam to drop a shot at the last.

The last hole at Hubbelrath is a par 4 played from one side of a valley to the other with the second shot hit up a steep hill to a green that slopes quite sharply back to front just below the clubhouse. As Sam teed off Mark McNulty had handed in his card and finished tied with Broadhurst. They would have to play off but I wondered how many of the German fans were aware of the drama of the Cup situation as it affected Darcy, James and Torrance as Sam came up the last. Only two of that three would make it to Kiawah. Torrance drove into the light rough on the left and then missed the green with his second shot. Significantly, however, he missed short and left, close enough for him to use that long extended putter, the one that had saved his career three years earlier, for his third shot. He putted up to three feet. The crowds on the green went silent as Sam adjusted the putter carefully under his chin and lined up the yard-long putt that would decide so much as far as the 1991 Cup team was concerned. He holed it.

The situation had been resolved. Darcy, who had started the day in seventh spot, had now been passed as well by Torrance and had dropped back into 10th spot. Broadhurst, who lost his play-off to McNulty, the result I am sure of relaxing after realizing that he had made the Ryder Cup team thanks to his string of tremendous performances in the final month of points collecting, culminating in his gutsy showing at Hubbelrath, was naturally delighted. So too

75

were Torrance and Gilford who, in the end, edged out Eamonn by a mere 58 points. This is how the final table looked:

1.	Seve BALLESTEROS	333,069
2.	Colin MONTGOMERIE	279,335
3.	Steven RICHARDSON	267,403
4.	Ian WOOSNAM	246,851
5.	Sam TORRANCE	193,738
6.	Bernhard LANGER	191,913
7.	Paul BROADHURST	185,503
8.	David FEHERTY	184,375
9.	David GILFORD	182,203
10.	Eamonn Darcy	182,145
11.	Jose Maria OLAZABAL	174,533
12.	Per-Ulrik Johansson	153,226
13.	Michael McLean	125,820
14.	Anders Forsbrand	123,890
15.	Nick FALDO	119,865
16.	Costantino Rocca	114,099
17.	Jose Rivero	110,446
18.	Miguel Angel Martin	105,734
19.	Barry Lane	104,189
20.	Peter Mitchell	100,674

It had taken over 182,000 points to make the side and Eamonn had missed out by the equivalent of a decimal point, because I was going to give my final wild cards to Olazabal, now 11th in the table, and to James. It was just one of those horrible things as far as Eamonn was concerned, a situation I wish I could have avoided. Still, my mind was made up, although I was aware the support for James had always assumed that Darcy would be in the team. In the circumstances, I wanted to have a quick talk to Bernhard Langer – one of the senior men – about my final choice of James, but discovered that he had left the course having, for once, not been in contention for the German title.

As I walked towards the clubhouse I bumped into my old Ryder Cup partner Brian Barnes. I had no need to but, with Eamonn Darcy very much on my mind, I decided to tell him about my decision to choose James. He agreed with what I was doing and I went into the clubhouse to mark time before heading off to the press conference where I was to reveal all. By chance I walked straight into Mark who was preparing to go to the airport with his wife Jane. I told him he was 'in'. I would say he looked more relieved than shocked. He had wanted so badly to go to Kiawah. I asked him to say nothing to anyone because I had not yet made the official announcement. He promised me that he would not let me down at Kiawah and I said I knew he would not.

The press conference to announce the side went well. I was not grilled about my selection of Mark James. Those reporters doing stories for Irish newspapers knew they had a sad one, but I felt I had done the best for the team. I believed that I had the perfect mix of experience and youth and I reckoned that I would be going to Kiawah with a team that was stronger in depth than recent teams had been.

As I flew home from Dusseldorf, the 26 weeks of points collecting over, I could not help but feel for Eamonn. When I had been appointed captain I had accepted the responsibilities of the post. I knew there would be tough decisions to take but that I must, at all times, do what I felt was best for the team. Voting for Faldo and for Olazabal and for James as my wild cards was in no way a reflection of how I felt about Darcy's play. I had three choices and as captain I had made them.

When I was back home at Wentworth I tried to contact Eamonn by telephone, without success. I did write to him, saying how sorry I was that the circumstances had contrived against him in Dusseldorf. Later Eamonn told Irish pressmen that I had known he was not going to Germany because he had planned a holiday that week with his children. I cannot remember him telling me that – and if he did, it did not alter the situation that there was always the slim chance that he might not make it and that he would not be given a wild card.

By not going to Germany Eamonn may have given some people the idea that he did not want to play in the Cup, but I know he wanted to be on the side just as desperately as Mark James, Sam Torrance, Per-Ulrik Johansson, Gordon Brand Jnr and Sandy Lyle, all of whom went to Germany. Eamonn may feel bitter for a time and I may no longer be one of his favourite people, but he is not the first player to be disappointed by such events and I am not the first captain to play the role of villain. In 1985 Tony Jacklin left Christy O'Connor Jnr out of the side in similar circumstances; they did not speak until Tony chose him as a wild card in 1989!

77

Seven of that 1989 side would be making the journey to Kiawah. Of the other five, Gordon Brand Jnr and Ronan Rafferty had come closest to selection. Gordon knew that he had his chance but failed to take it. I was disappointed that he had not made the team and was able to tell him the bad news prior to the Dusseldorf press conference. As for Ronan, I had always considered him to be one of the best players in the world, a tremendously talented performer. When he had helped us retain the Cup by beating Mark Calcavecchia in the singles at The Belfry in 1989, I thought that would be a turning point in his career as far as the Cup was concerned. He had made a very nervous start in that first Cup match but I remembered Tony Jacklin chatting to him, impressing on him the necessity just to play his own game. On the final day, he did and produced one of the key victories at a crucial time. At the start of the year he was one of the men I had expected to play a major role in defence of the Cup at Kiawah. It did not work out that way, although I hope Ronan will be back stronger than ever in 1993.

I had also hoped at the start of the year that Sandy Lyle, working so hard to sort out his game, would make the side but although there had been signs of him returning to form close to the end of the points-collecting period, he also missed out. Maybe he regrets now not having played more regularly at the start and in the middle of the season in Europe, but typically he took the disappointment well. I know he is determined to make a Cup comeback in 1993, even if The Belfry is not one of his favourite courses. I certainly was delighted when his dedication was rewarded with victory in the BMW International Open in Munich later in the year, a win that was applauded by thousands of golfers in Britain and around the world who had suffered with him through his slump.

The German Open ended on 25 August and the Ryder Cup was not scheduled to begin until 27 September so there was a month to finalize matters, tie up any loose ends and ensure all was in order. For instance, the tailors had to move smartly to measure up David Gilford and Paul Broadhurst for their team clothing. They had not been in the group measured up in late May.

An unusual problem arose when I learned that David Gilford was thinking of taking fellow Tour pro and close friend, Glenn Ralph, to Kiawah as his caddie in place of Martin Gray from

Worksop. Martin had only been working with him for a few weeks but had caddied for him when he won the English Open. I did not know what the Cup rule (if any) was regarding a fellow professional acting as caddie but I felt strongly enough to tell David that, while I would not force the issue, I would rather he took his Tour caddie. The idea of taking Glenn was a nice one, but my perception is that on Tour there are players and there are caddies and the division is clear. I remembered the reaction there was in 1987 when Jose Rivero decided not to take his regular caddie – Fanny Sunesson at the time – but instead to use his brother to carry his bag; or the murmurings when Jose Maria Olazabal used his manager Sergio Gomez as caddie at Muirfield Village. The other caddies did not like it. A caddie's job is very demanding. I wondered whether Glenn Ralph, one of the nicest fellows on Tour, would really have got up at dawn to plot the pins at Kiawah. Would a pro acting as a caddie be prepared to do all the little tasks that collectively ensure a player is comfortable on the course and has the chance to give of his best? Maybe, but the problem disappeared when David decided to stick with his Tour caddie. Frankly, I was glad he did.

Another incident more directly involved with the team created headlines. Seve made it known that he did not think it right that Bernhard Langer should play in the Far East during the week before the Ryder Cup and I cannot say I was overwhelmed to hear the news of his pre-Cup plans either. I did raise the matter of his punishing schedule with his manager, John Simpson, although aware that Bernhard is a most experienced traveller. He would, in due course, prove that his Far East jaunt did not adversely affect his play one bit.

79

6

Hype and More Hype

There have been occasions when the Ryder Cup side has travelled together as a team to the match but not this time. Bernhard Langer made his own way to Kiawah via Japan and a ninth-place finish in the ANA Sapporo Open, while Broadhurst and Torrance had left for America a week early to play in the BC Open. Both Paul, who had never played in the United States before, and David Gilford, whose one experience of competitive golf in America had been the Pine Valley Walker Cup, had requested invitations to the BC Open, urged on by Seve who felt the experience would be invaluable. Gilford was unlucky and did not gain a spot but Broadhurst did and on his debut in the States finished joint ninth – a factor I noted with considerable delight as I read the newspapers on the morning the rest of us were leaving from Heathrow. Sam missed the half-way cut.

We had congregated the night before at the Edwardian Hotel near Heathrow Airport but because of the confusion caused by the sudden collapse of the Keith Prowse company, who had been the PGA's ticket and travel agents for the Ryder Cup for several years, a champagne dinner arranged to introduce the team to the

Concorde patrons – the fans who wanted to travel to Kiawah in style with the team – had to be cancelled. That was disappointing for the patrons but, despite the initial uncertainty and confusion, they did at least get their Concorde trip. The plane was flying us all to Charleston after the PGA European Tour, the PGA and the team's sponsors, Johnnie Walker, had taken on the financial responsibility for the flight – a responsibility reduced considerably by the understanding executives at British Airways who gave us a special price.

Johnnie Walker had arranged a press conference on the Monday morning mainly for the television boys because most of the regular golf writers were already on their way to Kiawah or even there already. I was not much in favour of this conference because of the hassle it involved. It meant leaving the Concorde lounge, which was through customs, to go back to the interview room and then trooping back through customs again. I thought the players might not be too pleased about this and that a simple photocall would have done but I need not have worried. The players – eight of them because Seve Ballesteros did not fly into London until later that morning – happily co-operated. The press conference went well and everyone was in a cheery mood which pleased me. I recall Nick Faldo making the comment that the United States players could not come to terms with their Tour being rated second to ours if one took the results of recent Cup matches as the yardstick. That ensured a headline or two!

81

I do not know who did the seating plan on Concorde but I had a front seat and so did Seve. The plane was not full and the wives who were travelling with babies all had a spare seat beside them which was a luxury they had not expected. Keith Prowse had hoped to sell all the seats left after initially donating 40 to the official party. The Concorde patrons who were travelling with us were at the back of the plane and during the short flight to New York I thanked all of them for their support and hoped that they would enjoy the Ryder Cup as much as the team hoped to do. Most of the players had travelled by Concorde before but they enjoyed a visit to the cockpit at one of the take-offs or landings. We went down in New York because Concorde could not fly direct to Charleston and that enabled us to go through customs. What a delight that was compared to the experience we had had in 1971 at St Louis. That year we were shunted around and had to clear customs in a shed at the far end of the airport. I remember it took an age, with the customs people going through everything and giving the impression they were not all that pleased to see us. This time it was different; the customs men and women could not have been more helpful and friendly – many of them were golfers! It was clear that the Ryder Cup match – or matches as the Americans prefer to call it or them – was now a much bigger affair in America than it had ever been before.

We were about an hour and a quarter on the ground and then it was off to Kiawah. The pilot had been given permission to circle the golf course before landing in Charleston. Looking out of the window it was easy to see how the course had been built on a nar-row raised sliver of land between the ocean and the swamp. It looked to be in tremendous shape. I had last seen it in its much rawer state a year earlier. The officials at the PGA of America had promised that the course would be immaculate on the week and from 8000 feet it seemed they had kept their word.

On the flight we had the normal up-front crew – a captain, a co-pilot and a flight engineer – but we also had a 'social' captain on board telling us what was happening throughout the trip. He provided an informative commentary about the plane and flight, explaining what was happening, for instance, when we felt that little surge when the plane burst through the sound barrier and began to fly supersonically – something it could not do on the second leg from New York to Charleston because of the US Federal Air Administration regulations.

As we were heading for the airport there was a minor alarm, although we were never in danger. The 'social' captain told us that the landing gear was being lowered. I listened for it and never heard it. Concorde comes in quite fast, not like a jumbo jet which seems to hover and hang over the runway for a time before touching down. Suddenly we were no longer at 6000 feet and descending, we were back up at 10,000 feet and climbing to circle the airport again. We had had to abort because the hydraulics operating the landing gear had failed. It was as well we did not know, as we went round again, that the pilot was lowering the wheels by hand but the second sweep did give the hundreds of people lining the airport perimeter another unplanned opportunity to marvel at Concorde's sleekness and style. The touchdown second time round was perfect and we glided up to the stand only to find, not surprisingly, that it did not fit Concorde.

It took some time to take the luggage off and then I lined up the players to go through as a team rather than one by one. We were delighted that there were a considerable number of British and Irish supporters to meet us plus Spaniards and, I have no doubt, Germans too. The welcoming party was cheerfully noisy and enthusiastic with many of the fans patriotically waving flags. I even spotted two toddlers with little flags doing their share of waving. It was marvellous for us to feel so much at home. What was really nice, too, was that Dave Stockton had come along to the airport to welcome us. After doing some television interviews we were shepherded into the fleet of private cars that had been laid on to take us to Kiawah. Each player had his own car and, to begin with, a driver to ensure there would be no accidents en route from the airport to the course – a journey of about 45 minutes. Soon we were bowling along the dual-carriageway south and east towards Kiawah and Lesley and I could not help but notice how many of the shops on our route were flying huge American flags.

83

After about 20 minutes the cavalcade turned off into Main Road, something of a misnomer because it is more like a country road. We went over a bridge minutes before it opened to let some small craft through and continued past modest homes dotted around in the flat areas between the trees. The trees were huge. Indeed, there is an Angel Oak in the Kiawah area which they reckon is 400 years old and whose branches are so long and heavy they sag down to the ground. Closer to the course we headed into more thickly wooded country and noticed that many of the lower branches of the trees hanging over the road had been chopped down. This had been done to enable a specially hired fleet of 250 Greyhound-type buses and their drivers, brought in from other States, to ferry spectators to and from Charleston and Kiawah for the match. The last two miles to the entrance of the course had been converted into a dual-carriageway since my last visit in order to make the transportation operation run even more smoothly – and it did all week.

The villas provided for us down by the ocean and away from everyone else were beautiful and the team and I spent the next hour unpacking and settling in. We had arrived too late for the players to have a first look at the course but I was not too concerned about that. There was plenty of time. We met up with Paul, Sam, who had played the Ocean course and was able to give the team a detailed view of the difficulties he had encountered on it, and Bernhard, who had managed to keep a frighteningly tight intercontinental schedule and flown in from Japan. Now we were a team and there was a good spirit among us as we headed off to our first function, happily an informal one.

Dave Stockton had arranged a welcome barbeque at nearby Mingo Point. It was a players-only evening, a very private party to bring everyone together and to underline that the Ryder Cup was a competition started to foster goodwill between golfers on both sides of the Atlantic. Friendship had been the initial raison d'etre for the match and we had a lovely evening, marred only by the voracity of the mosquitos which forced some of us to leave early. That informal party at Mingo Point gave us a very pleasant start to a week in which the pressure would grow in intensity day by day.

As far as I know we all slept well and we were up early for the only full team press conference of the week. What a shambles it was. The PGA of America officials had decided, unknown to me, that the conference should be what they called a locker-room type of get-together in which the players would mingle with the pressmen instead of having questions fired at them on a dais. I had been asked to delay this conference until after we had played but it was too late to change the programme. Anyway that first press conference was chaotic. The PGA of America was not ready for it and I got very angry indeed. Eventually I had to organize it myself. The conference went badly in my opinion because, as we all stood around, I noticed the journalists and radio men were cornering the star players – Seve, in particular. He was getting most of the attention because of his reputation and I could see a danger of some players being left out of it. I decided this was not good enough. Taking nothing away from Seve, I considered that the way things were going it was bad for team morale and, anyway, it was not how I had planned it. I called the team up on to the platform to answer

84

questions and even then it was not a great success because the microphone was not working properly. When the American team had their conference later in the day it was organized the way I had had to reorganize my one. The American officials had known for six months in advance when I would be bringing my team in but had made a complete hash of it. What a start!

My game plan for the first day had been to let the players do exactly what they wanted to do – play the course or go to the practice range to work out with their coaches. I knew I did not need to tell them how to prepare but I had indicated that I would have official practice on the Wednesday and Thursday when I would try out several pairings to see how they worked.

I had to change the plan, however, when I realized that most of the team wanted to get on the course. So I decided to pair them off on that first day because I believed it would look bad if they went off individually – Nick at eight o'clock, Woosie at nine, Sam and David at ten. That, I reckoned, would give the wrong impression – the impression that we were not a team. I did not like making changes because I always like to follow a plan through but I made up three fourballs, stressing there was no special significance in the groupings. I included Mark James although he had told his caddie he would chip and putt a bit and, later, go to the range. I knew he would not be going out on the course but I was slow to appreciate that by saying nothing in the press room about Mark's individual plans, the European journalists, for whom the first press conference had been arranged, would wonder what was wrong with James when they spotted later that he was not with Ian Woosnam, Dave Feherty and Sam Torrance. There was, of course, nothing wrong with him. He was going along with what I had originally planned the day to be but I was quickly approached on the course by various sportswriters wondering if Mark was injured or ill. I should have realized this would happen. It was my mistake and it caused a minor stir. That apart, the practice went well and the players realized what they would have to face up to on Pete Dye's Ocean course!

From the moment we had arrived at Kiawah, it had been impossible to ignore the American hype. The fans – and most of them naturally were American – wore stars-and-stripes shirts or tee-shirts with the message emblazoned across the chest or back, 'The Cup

85

belongs in the US' or 'Our turn now'. In the trade tents most of the sporting apparel had American flags on it or some other pro-American logo. I knew I would need to caution the players about over-reacting to any incidents that might occur during the match. American fans are naturally boisterous and jumpy and generally lack the sophistication of the British fan except when riled. I remembered back in 1969 how the Ken Still and Dave Hill incidents got out of hand at Birkdale as the crowds took our side against the American antics. The pressure and tension of the match would be considerable and might, from time to time, spill over which was why it was essential we must always remain controlled. Ignorance of the rules in tense situations could have explosive consequences but we tried to cover this with an extensive rules get-together later that afternoon with the Americans. At that meeting it was decided that all sandy areas would be treated as waste areas, even the sand traps. There was so much sand around it would have been too complicated in some instances to decide what was a bunker, where you could not ground your club under the rules of golf, and what was a waste area, where you could ground it without penalty. In the circumstances it was more sensible to designate all sand as waste area. We were all in agreement.

We also had a long discussion about the use of different balls in foursomes, ending with the logical decision that the usual US Tour one-ball rule be applied. In other words, a player teeing up on the first would continue to play with that compression and make of ball at all the odd holes where he had the honour. His partner could use a different compression and make of ball at the even holes but the balls could not be switched around. In most cases it was likely that both players would be playing the same compression ball anyway, so there would be no problem, but it was best to talk it through just in case. The compression of a ball – a measure of how tight the rubber is wound around the central core – is more important to players in America where the greens are usually soft and holding and it is useful to be able to spin the ball back towards the hole. The job is made easier by the use of a 100-compression ball that flies lower than the 90-compression one. Here in Britain we do not play so-called target golf so much and the need to back-spin shots is not as important, although spectators are always very impressed when they see us do it. The meeting was a thorough affair. Officials were determined no team member would be in any doubt about what to do if there was a dispute nor would they be in any doubt about the rules – or so they hoped!

In an ideal world there would be no incidents at Kiawah but instinct told me that, no matter how much we tried to avoid them, they would occur with the Americans trying desperately hard to win back the Cup and our players equally keen not to give it back. At one of our earliest team get-togethers in the villa I further emphasized the point that if there was any problem that looked as if it might develop into something controversial the official game referee should be called and, if it was a major confrontation or dispute, I should be at the scene. Naturally I hoped there would not be any on-course trouble because every two years at the Ryder Cup we golfers have the chance to prove to the world that it is possible to compete at the highest level in the most sporting manner. I hoped nothing would detract from that.

Although I felt I would have enough control over any incidents that cropped up involving the players of both sides, I was more worried about incidents involving players and spectators, especially with Dave Stockton whipping up national fervour to the extent that the official US team uniform included a camouflage cap of a type not unlike that used by Stormin' Norman in the Gulf War. The last thing we needed at Kiawah were committed spectators shouting at the top of a player's backswing or clapping and cheering wildly when one of our men missed a putt or hit an approach shot into a bunker. Some of the less experienced American players, I remembered, had been critical of the British crowds at The Belfry in 1985, claiming they were biased then in our favour, but I have always insisted that they were never so. Excited for us yes, because we looked like winning for the first time since 1957, but not to the extent that they treated the American players unfairly. It is tough not to be nationalistic but most sports fans are all for fair play. Golf, thankfully, has been sheltered from the boorish lager-lout behaviour that is a major problem in other sports and to some extent the spectators at Kiawah had as much a responsibility as the players to uphold the honour of the game.

As far as the team were concerned, we must not allow ourselves

87

to be provoked and we must be gracious losers if things did not happen to go our way. I have always been philosophic about defeat and wanted my team to be too. They all knew that it was possible to play to the very best of their capabilities but on the day lose to someone who happened to play even better. That is golf, and they had been there before. I always recall the time at Augusta in 1975 when Tom Weiskopf, who wanted so badly to win a Masters Green Jacket, played as well as he was physically and mentally able to do but in the end lost out to Jack Nicklaus. I remember reading reports of him sitting in the press room asking himself aloud what he had to do to win. He had given everything and could not believe that he had not won. There would be players at Kiawah who would give everything and lose and if and when they did, I wanted ours to be the first to shake the hands of the winners.

The match, played in what was going to be as charged-up an atmosphere as the last day of the Open or the Masters, would be a severe test for some of the five rookies in the side but they must put everything into perspective. They must remember that it was all part of the learning process, something that might turn out to be quite unpleasant but which they had to experience on the way to the top. It might be frightening this time but it would not be so bad in future Ryder Cups. I wanted to do everything I could, however, to let them enjoy the occasion and impressed on them that even though they might feel unwell, have knots in their stomachs or find themselves with sweaty palms, that was a natural reaction. They had played themselves into the side, proving, in the process, that they were the best in Europe and certainly as good as if not better than the opposition. This did not mean being over-confident, just realistic about their status in the match. They were good players and there was no reason why this should not be reflected in their producing the result we wanted – a win.

The Ryder Cup is such a special team occasion. In these mercenary times, it is perhaps anachronistic that no one gets paid to play in the Cup but that is the way the players on both sides of the Atlantic want it to remain. The match itself may generate millions of dollars – an estimated 10 million this time – but it is the one week every two years when pride and patriotism, not financial gain, is the motivating force. Of course the team members benefit indirectly because some of the profit from the matches held in Europe is channelled back into tournament prize funds. Ryder Cup status probably also helps players negotiate better long-term contracts, but it is right and proper that no one gets paid appearance money to turn up and play in the match. In this respect the Cup is unique in international sport and golf is proud of that.

The unofficial practice on that first day went well. It was really a get-your-bearings day but what pleased me was that the team did not have any huge misgivings about the course and no one was badly out of form. Ian Woosnam called the course unique and when talking to American reporters David Feherty, always a live-wire, said that the course reminded him of Mars rather than Scotland or Ireland. We knew the course would be the same for both teams and that there would be a premium on hitting the greens. The players were not surprised at what they found because I had explained the Ocean course to them, but they realized that if the wind blew really strongly the course might not be as fair a test of golf as Dye had planned it to be. Still, it was in good condition with the fairways like lush carpets which you could imagine the greenkeepers rolling back to brush away loose sand.

On our first full day at Kiawah, it was inevitable for Stockton to latch on to a news agency report from London, claiming that Nick Faldo and Ian Woosnam had indicated that the problem with the Americans was that they were no longer number one in golf but that they could not quite bring themselves to believe it. The local press loved the comment, allegedly made by Seve, that the US team lacked on-course leadership. Dave played the headlines game, too, pointing to Irwin, Floyd and Wadkins as natural leaders. He said he could not believe what the European players were saying and continued constantly to query whether the European team could get to know the Ocean course and all its subtleties in just three days. Interestingly Raymond Floyd had admitted to me that the course was playing very differently in Cup week from the course he had played on previous occasions.

I rather agreed with Nick who told another group of American reporters that the Ryder Cup was a great sporting event, not just a great golf match, and that we could all do without the excess hype which the Americans were creating. Seve weighed in, too, with a

89

reminder that despite what Jack Nicklaus had said a couple of days earlier about the Cup match being a war, it was nothing of the sort. It was simply a competition between two sides to see who is better. David Feherty, pointing out that there was no acrimony between the European and American sides, added that the Ryder Cup was simply a celebration of the game. Yet you could not help but feel the Americans were so pumped up about the whole thing that if their team did lose – and I still felt that we had the side to beat them – the nation would be devastated! After all the preparation they had put in, and after all Dave Stockton's efforts to create the kind of team spirit the Europeans had enjoyed in 1985, 1987 and 1989, to lose would be nothing short of a national disaster for them. I kept quiet. I had enough on my mind thinking about my team and how I would pair them off than to worry about responding – on the Tuesday at any rate. However, I did move quickly the next day to deny Stockton's continuing suggestion that we were not properly prepared.

Back in our villas, which were lovely but I noted not quite so good as the American team's headquarters, we relaxed before the first function of the week, the president's dinner – where the PGA of America's chief executive Jim Autrey said grace and used it to pray for an American victory. We sat in stunned silence! They really were worried they might not win. It is traditional that in addition to the two PGAs giving each other's official party presents, the two captains exchange gifts between the teams. I gave the Americans a Waterford Crystal bowl and they gave us a crystal shell – the logo of the resort. Our PGA gave each of the Americans a carriage clock and we received pewter cigarette boxes. It was a pleasant enough evening but all the time, in the back of my mind, I was thinking of the match and my pairings and waiting for the unexpected to happen that might cause me completely to alter my plans.

90

7

Properly Prepared

I did not sleep all that well that second night. I was concerned about 91 whether I had got everything right, but that was not the real problem. What woke me was another indication of the hype American fans will go to when they feel their players have their backs to the wall. A Charleston disc jockey got into what he considered the gung-ho Ryder Cup spirit by calling our rooms at Kiawah on a 'Wake up the enemy' mission. He had offered $100 to any listener who knew the telephone numbers of our villas and someone at Kiawah, keen to get the cash, had given him them.

It was childish, but apart from making my disgust known to Dave Stockton and the officials of the PGA of America I said nothing and was not prepared to make an issue of it. I felt it was best to cope with it and carry on as if nothing had happened, advising the players to take their telephones off the hook at night to avoid any early calls. I kept my phone operational in case a player wanted to contact me for any reason. Nick Faldo had an early-morning call, Paul Broadhurst was disturbed and I got a call in the middle of the night and then a continuing series of calls where the person at the other end hung up as soon as I answered. The disc jockey, Michael D, was asked whether he was concerned that his actions would be construed as most unsportsmanlike, but he just did not care. His attitude was that it was fair game to do anything that might help the American team win. It was an obnoxious thing to have happened and in a way pathetic but apart from one or two of the team or their wives being inconvenienced the matter was quickly forgotten. Inevitably, it made the headlines in the British papers and BBC Radio even hit back by phoning Michael D at four in the morning.

In our team meeting I had discussed foursomes and the fact that for some reason or another we seldom seemed to do well in this form of golf. In Tony's day we had practised foursomes on only one of the nines, usually on the final practice day, but I decided that we should play nine holes of fourball games and nine holes of foursomes each day. It was imperative that we got off to a good start and I had told the team that it was my intention to play what I considered the strongest four pairings from the practice days on that first morning. Of course there is such a difference between foursomes and fourballs that I knew that some players would have a preference for one form or another, although I knew they would play where and when I wanted them to. In the fourball matches you need players who are going to make birdies. They may drop shots along the way, too, but birdies are the key. In foursomes you are looking for players whose game is consistent in that they are hitting fairways and, more importantly, greens in regulation. Winning in foursomes was about making fewest mistakes.

The official groupings the previous day of Nick Faldo, Bernhard Langer, Steven Richardson and Colin Montgomerie; Severiano Ballesteros, Jose Maria Olazabal, Paul Broadhurst and David Gilford; and Ian Woosnam, Sam Torrance and David Feherty – Mark James had not played – had no real significance, but on the first full practice day I had decided that the more experienced couples should play with the rookies. It came as no surprise, I am sure, to the press when I once again had Ballesteros and Olazabal (who had won 3½ points out of 4 at The Belfry in 1989 and 3 out of 4 at Muirfield Village in 1987) together again, and this time paired up Nick Faldo and Ian Woosnam whose record was equally impressive as a partnership – five wins, two halved games and only one defeat in the last two matches.

The idea of the second day pairings was to give me the opportunity to put together some players who might gel. We played fourballs on the front nine, foursomes on the back. I put Nick and Ian with Colin Montgomerie and Paul Broadhurst; Mark James and Bernhard Langer, a previous Cup pairing, with Steven Richardson and David Gilford; and I had the Spaniards with Sam and David. The idea was to ascertain who was playing best and put the best players on the course at the same time without making them play too much golf on the first two days and tiring them for the singles. It is always a tricky juggling business. What was impressing me as I supervised the practice was that all the players were in form. Certainly Ian Woosnam was trying out several putters but I hoped he would find the right one to help him produce his best on the putting surfaces that were so different in texture to those we play in Europe.

With the exception of Olazabal and Gilford, the players all had coaches with them. It was something I had encouraged and we had helped make arrangements for them to come to Kiawah. They were busy that morning running the rule over their boys. Bob Torrance, Sam's dad, looks after David Feherty, Ian Woosnam and, of course, Sam. David Leadbetter was helping Nick Faldo, whom I could see even this early in the week was uncomfortable on the greens, and Seve, whom he had assisted back to his best form with a timely chat in Japan earlier in the year. He had suggested then a little swing change and a small putting switch and, armed with his new Tad Moore putter in place of the Ping he had used for 15 years, Seve had come roaring back and would go on to finish European No. 1 for the sixth time. Gavin Christie has long looked after Mark James. Steven Richardson – like Sam, the son of a pro – had his father John in close attendance. Colin Montgomerie had brought Bill Fergusson, formerly pro at Ilkley, to ensure there was nothing wrong with his swing and Bernhard Langer had Willi Hofmann with him. Not to be outdone, Paul Broadhurst had brought along Frank Miller, a retired professional from the Robin Hood Club with whom he has worked for many years.

The players worked hard that morning getting to know the course even better. Seve had a bit of a cold but the team had no

93

other health problems. I knew we had a fit, strong team with all of them ready to play. On the previous day, as a result I think of jet-lag and the hot sun, some players had had headaches and sweated a bit, but today we were better able to handle the conditions in our lightweight gear. Nick, as always, looked and probably was the fittest. It is amazing how he eats like a horse but never gets fat. We hardly stopped for lunch, just snatched a few sandwiches or pasta in the trailer. Things were going well.

As the team tackled Kiawah again I went into the press tent twice to nail a rumour that had been niggling me and, more importantly, the team. What I said needed to be said. Having read the morning papers I told the European press in the morning and the American newspapermen in the afternoon that there seemed to be a sugges-tion that somehow we had undermined our chances by not coming earlier to practise. I explained that our side had not been finalized until a month before and that it was, logistically, not easy for play-ers to opt out of the lucrative Volvo Tour. I indicated I was offended at what had been written and pointed out that I could not remem-ber any American golfers coming over prior to the first of The Belfry matches to get to know the course. They got the message and in the process some pressmen also assumed that Dave Stockton and I were not getting on behind the scenes.

Nothing was further from the truth, but people sometimes inter-pret comments in the wrong way. For instance, when talking about beating Dave in the 1971 Ryder Cup match I said that when he holed the putt on the last green to halve with me he acted as if he had won the US Open. That was construed as a veiled criticism of him by me. When I was asked whether the course was as tiring for me as Stockton had said it was for him, I had jocularly pointed out, quite correctly, that I was younger than Dave and trained more than him. That was perceived as yet another dig by me at the US cap-tain. To be fair, Dave was trying to cool things down himself now, telling the press in his interview that all the 'War on the Shore' business was being blown out of proportion. Apparently he said that he just wanted his players, an 'awesome group', to relax and concentrate on beating the damned course. His desire, he said, was to have captained a side that would walk away on Sunday night with memories that would last a lifetime. This had been his line a year earlier and I still agreed, but I wanted the European memories to be sweeter than the American ones!

The practice had to be finished early on Wednesday to give us time to prepare for the big Ryder Cup Gala Dinner being staged in Charleston that night. It promised to be a glittering occasion staged on the day that *Scarlett* – the sequel to *Gone with the Wind* – was published and sold out in hours. Margaret Mitchell had written the original book, turned into that marvellous film staring Clark Gable and Vivien Leigh, and the Mitchell estate had chosen a Charleston lady, Alexandra Ripley, to produce the sequel. The first edition amounted to 700,000 copies.

Sadly the dinner would turn out to be a damp squib because of an accident on the way to the function in which the American player Steve Pate injured his abdomen when the limousine in which he was travelling with Corey Pavin was involved in a crash. It was caused by another car stopping too quickly in order to allow a new police escort team from the city to move out and take over from the county boys. Several cars were involved in the smash and Bernhard Langer was in one of them although he was not injured. I was in the lead car with Lesley and Dave and Cathy Stockton and we and the rest of my team arrived at the Omni Hotel in the middle of Charleston on schedule . . . then waited and waited for the rest to arrive. Clearly something was wrong. Then we heard there had been an accident and that it seemed a serious one. The initial reports were that Steve had been removed to intensive care and that Corey Pavin's wife was also in a bad way. Dave Stockton was getting grim news from the hospital where Lanny Wadkins and Raymond Floyd and their wives had gone with the injured. Inside the hall the guests in their ball gowns and dinner suits had been waiting for an hour. There was a cloud hanging over the occasion although the news filtering back began to get better. Pate was not as bad as had been at first expected but there was still a worrying uncertainty in the air. Finally it was decided we should go in and dinner was served.

Dick Smith, the tall PGA of America president, was master of ceremonies at the dinner and as we were coming to the end of the meal he announced that we would now see a celebration of the Ryder Cup over the years. It was a history of matches from the

95

American angle only. All their top players were seen in action, none of ours. The video had been made by NBC Television for promotional purposes and as far as I recall it ended in 1983, the last time the Americans had won the match, and then only by a point. We neither saw nor heard of Sir Henry Cotton, Dai Rees, Max Faulkner, Christy O'Connor Snr, Fred Daly – just a few of the people who have played key roles in the match for us over the years.

There were plenty of sarcastic comments flying around among my team, I can tell you, and if it had not been such a sombre evening I would have made reference to the biased footage when I introduced the players. It was neither the time nor the occasion to underscore the Americans' lack of tact and bad taste. They had shown little of the goodwill Samuel Ryder had been so keen to foster. We were all disappointed and it highlighted a curious naivety in the Cup arrangements. Lanny Wadkins later came to me and said he hoped a proper letter of apology would be forthcoming from the American PGA.

Nobody had made reference to the accident but when I got up to speak I felt I needed to say something and just made the point that my team, the European officials and I all wished Steve Pate and Mrs Shannon Pavin speedy recoveries from the injuries they had received in the car crash. The guests gasped at the news. I was on my way back to my seat when I glanced over and, to my surprise, saw Shannon, having scoffed her Layered Seafood Terrine with Papaya Chile relish, tucking into her Medallions of Veal with Pesto Cream and Romaine Salad with Julienne of Tri-coloured Peppers, shredded Danish Havarti Cheese, Toasted Croutons and Parmesan Peppercorn Dressing!

The entertainment that evening was provided by the Gatlin Brothers, one of the most famous groups of the American entertainment world. Larry Gatlin was making a comeback after having a throat operation but, under the circumstances, he cut his show to just a few songs and we all slipped away.

Later it was discovered that Steve Pate had been detained for a check up, that nothing had been broken or damaged internally in the accident but that he had received considerable bruising. His participation in the match was uncertain and as we went to bed that night I wondered if Stockton might bring in his first reserve, Tim

The 18th hole on Pete Dye's Ocean course may have looked for all the world as if it had been transported from a British seaside links but how deceptive looks can be. Kiawah was an American course by the sea. The hole looks tranquil enough on this calm day but in a testing breeze it proved far tougher than I initially imagined it would be, and a heartbreak too. It was here on the last day that a couple of inches would decide who held the Cup for the next two years and where Bernhard Langer faced up to the ultimate in golfing pressure.

An aerial view of Pete Dye's signature hole, the 197-yards 17th over water to a two-tiered green – a green made more difficult to hit in the left-to-right wind blowing into the players' faces during the three days of the match. Downwind in practice, Bernhard Langer holed using a 6-iron!

Paul Azinger playing the 17th in the afternoon fourballs on the second day against Ian Woosnam and Paul Broadhurst . . . and it was from a wicked lie in the sand to the left of the green that Woosnam played a brilliant recovery to give him and Broadhurst victory over Azinger and Irwin.

Colin Montgomerie, backed up by Mark James and Steve Richardson, led the cheers at the 17th when the Spaniards squared against Payne Stewart and Mark Calcavecchia and 20 minutes later, in the fading light, Seve and Ollie had maintained their unbeaten record. In 12 games in three Ryder Cup matches the inspired pair have only lost once.

101

Seve found himself waist-high in the sea oats at one hole but emerged unbeaten on the week while Nick Faldo, despite a fright or two on the back nine, did exactly what I asked him to do by winning the top single against Raymond Floyd. David Feherty relished the chance to snatch a point from US Open champion Payne Stewart, but poor David Gilford, seen here on the Saturday, could only look on, his chance of a singles game snatched away when Steve Pate withdrew.

102

When you have been five down and still earn a half point you are entitled, like Colin Montgomerie after his match with Mark Calcavecchia, to be reasonably pleased – but as the hours went by it became more difficult to pinpoint where the vital points would come from and my wife Lesley and former captain Tony Jacklin could not help me! The defeat of Cup hero Jose Maria Olazabal by Paul Azinger was a particularly bitter blow. The expression on his face says it all.

The tremendous courage of Bernhard Langer enabled him to keep his vital deciding match with three-times US Open champion Hale Irwin alive and had us biting our nails right to the end, but it was Irwin who celebrated in champagne. Langer's efforts did not go unnoticed by the European fans who cheered him to the roof when he visited the hospitality tents after the match.

Seve said he would have missed it. Tony Jacklin would not have wanted to be in Bernhard Langer's shoes on that final green and I said no-one should be put under that kind of pressure at the end of three hard tiring days of golf. Bernhard had holed two tough putts in the closing holes to take his match with Irwin down to the last, but fate would deal an unkind cut to a man who has recovered three times from putting yips. The silence as he putted was eerie. The relief of the Americans when the putt missed the hole and they knew the Cup was theirs was overwhelming. The distress the team and all the European fans felt for Bernhard at that moment was immense as the ball lay two cruel inches from the hole. In defeat we were more determined than ever to win the Cup back in 1993 and I was delighted when the courageous Langer bounced back to win his own tournament – the Mercedes German Masters – the following week.

Simpson, who had finished just outside the automatic top 10. I might have, ever so casually, pondered Stockton's problem but Dave had made up his mind. The official reason given the next day was that it was too late to bring in a reserve to play the Ocean course, but I regarded Stockton as unwilling to bring in, at this stage, another person when so much team spirit had been engendered among the existing 12. If Pate was, in the end, unable to play then it might have the effect of making the remaining 11 try even harder, much as the loss of a player in soccer sometimes makes the remaining 10 footballers play above themselves. I also knew that if he did not play at all, then one of my team would have to sit out the singles.

As far as my team was concerned there had been no crises. We were all getting on well. No one was complaining and everyone was throwing himself into the business of preparing for what some people now call the fifth major. The efforts of some players in the team room were outstanding, but I am not going to single out those who were simply marvellous in the days leading up to and during the match. We were, after all, a team and a happy one at that. That night I slept well.

There was just one day of practice to go and I decided to try to provoke my leading two pairings into producing their best in the final foursomes and fourballs practice so I matched Seve and Ollie with Nick and Ian. I have to say the plan backfired a bit because Olazabal was playing so well. At the turn Woosnam and Faldo were on two under par but losing and did not much care for it. The Spaniards were five under after nine in the fourballs. I had put out David Feherty and Sam Torrance together with Bernhard Langer and Mark James – the next two strongest pairings I had. David and Sam were good friends and I knew they could make a lot of birdies together. Sam has always been a good team man. He is cheery and dedicated and just good to have around and I knew he would be a steadying influence for David on his debut. That meant the youngsters going out together – initially Steve Richardson and Colin Montgomerie and David Gilford and Paul Broadhurst, but after nine holes I switched Montgomerie and Broadhurst, when we turned to foursomes.

All the players, as I expected, were ready and willing to do what-

105

ever was required of them but I had chatted individually with them to ascertain just what their preferences were – foursomes or four-balls – so that I had enough information at my disposal when I sat down to choose the players for the first series – always foursomes. Steven Richardson and Paul Broadhurst both felt they were better fourball than foursomes players. I knew, too, that there were some players I would want to use all the time if possible – Seve Ballesteros, Jose Maria Olazabal, Mark James, whose fitness had also influenced me when I gave him the final wild card, Nick Faldo and Ian Woosnam. I anticipated Bernhard Langer would play four of the five series but I was also committed to playing everyone at least once before the final-day singles which I considered the crucial series.

Having to leave four people out in each of the first four series creates a problem. You have so many alternatives that your mind is buzzing with ideas of how best to place them on the day, taking into account their form, their level of confidence and their compatibility. Sometimes the most unlikely pairings turn out to be winning partnerships despite the fact that, on the face of it, the players are opposites. Sometimes the partnerships that seem tailor-made to do the job just do not work. I admit chemistry plays a big part in the success or failure of partnerships but I have always been of the view that players do not necessarily need to get on well together off the course for them to win points on it. All they are being asked to do is go out and do a job as professionally as they know how. Take Nick and Ian, a partnership that worked so well in the previous two matches. Ian has admitted that playing with Nick, who is so very steady, helps him play his naturally aggressive game more easily and maybe some of Ian's attacking attitude has rubbed off on Nick. During the practice I could see that Nick, who had been having problems with his putting all year, was having more trouble than most in getting to grips with the Bermuda-grass greens and that it was beginning to get him down. He had come to Kiawah determined to have a good Ryder Cup. He had not won a major in 1991 and had prepared and practised hard for the match. The fact was, however, that no matter how hard he tried to sort out his putting, the ball was just refusing to go into the hole. This sometimes happens. I could see he was lacking a little in inspiration but I was sure that he was still going to be a Cup winner, particularly in the four-somes and singles, because of his rock-solid play through the green on what was a very difficult course.

In some respects I felt that he was so determined to play his part for the team that he was trying too hard to get things right. We expect a lot from our superstars. The public look for them to get five points in the Cup match but they cannot always hit peak form at the press of the button, no matter how well they prepare. They are also usually playing against the best the Americans can produce. Curiously, Woosnam was also having putting problems – some-thing that affects every golfer from time to time. It is remarkable how a golfer's confidence is affected by his form on the greens. We have seen how inspirational Woosie can be when his putter is work-ing for him, as it did at the Masters earlier in the year. His talent is enormous and he has considerable courage, but what a debilitating effect poor form on the greens can have even on a player of his capability. Still I knew that in both Nick's and Ian's case something might just click into place – a minor adjustment to their grip, their method, their stance over the ball on the green – before the off to give their confidence a boost. Sometimes the difference between success and failure in golf is centimetres. I was never in any two minds about playing them together again on the first day.

107

The form on that final practice day dictated my first-day four-somes pairings and I made one change to the plan I had been working on. With the Spaniards and Nick and Ian as my banker pairings, I was looking for two others. In an effort to get us away to a fast start I paired Bernhard Langer with Mark James and, because I knew their preferences, I had to play either Paul Broadhurst or, more likely, Steven Richardson, who was hitting a fair number of loose shots but also making a lot of birdies, with Mark in the afternoon. I was looking for one more foursomes pair-ing. I knew I could play Sam Torrance and David Feherty on the first morning, but I decided to keep them fresh for the afternoon fourballs, which left me with Colin Montgomerie, David Gilford and Paul Broadhurst to choose from. Colin and David were both straight hitters and good putters and because I knew the value of consistency in foursomes I decided to give them my vote. They were playing well and had teamed up well together on the final nine holes of practice. What I would try to do was 'hide' them – if that is possible when there are only four games a series for the first two days. I put them in third place in the draw.

As the players completed their practice and headed for the mobile caravan that was our team room, spirits were high. The players felt they knew the course well enough and over a late lunch before the opening ceremony I told them of my plans. Seve and Ollie would lead off followed by Bernard and Mark. Colin and David would go third and Nick and Ian would play fourth. I felt that whomsoever the Americans put in against us we would come out all right with that line-up, even if I knew I was taking a gamble in putting two rookies together that first morning. They had told me that they felt they could handle it. Colin had admitted he did feel a little nervous but not so nervous it would affect his game. Gilford, the quiet man of the group, said he felt comfortable with the situation. I had no worries about them because I remembered how, on my own debut in 1969, I was just eager to get out and at the Americans. I was not nervous then and frankly saw no reason for Monty or David to be either. There comes a time – and this was it for both of them – when a golfer has to test himself by handling the ultimate in pressure. Their career prize winnings had proved they could do that and, with nothing to lose, I wanted them to enjoy the experience and win a point.

As luck would have it, when Dave Stockton announced his pairings Montgomerie and Gilford had been drawn against one of the Americans' most experienced partnerships, two of the over-40s – Lanny Wadkins, whom I respected as a great Cup fighter, and Hale Irwin, three times US Open champion. Dave Stockton revealed that Irwin was not his original choice for this pairing. He had planned on playing the injured Steve Pate five times and that on this occasion Pate would have partnered Wadkins had he been fit. Pate had bad bruising and having been released from hospital he had been treated through the night at 1.00, 3.00 and 6.00 in the American team headquarters by their own physiotherapist. He had managed to get to the course during the day to practise putt and walked on the dunes but Stockton had indicated, as I had anticipated, that although Pate was out of first-day action and might not play at all he would not be bringing in a reserve.

If there was a certain predictability about my opening line-up, the same could be said about Dave's. He had given Chip Beck a wild card because he knew his value as a partner to Paul Azinger. They had beaten Gordon Brand Jnr and Sam and then Nick and Ian at The Belfry in 1989 and he put them first, which meant they were in against Seve and Olazabal. Seve had played Azinger at The Belfry in the singles two years earlier and lost to him in reasonably controversial circumstances. Azinger, at the last, had been allowed to drop generously after drawing his tee shot into the lake. Seve, from an awkward lie on the edge of the sand trap on the outside corner of the dog-leg, had hit his second into the water. No putts had been given in that match. Both Seve and 'the Zinger', as he is known in the States, were dedicated to beating each other.

Stockton chose as his second foursomes pairing Fred Couples, who had not been a success at The Belfry in 1989 and was out to prove something to his critics and himself at Kiawah, with Ray Floyd and that was no surprise. I was happy that Mark and Bernhard, showing no signs of jet-lag after the long flight from Japan, could handle them. In the bottom game Ian and Nick, ranked respectively numbers one and three in the world, would have a good chance of beating Payne Stewart, the US Open champion, and Mark Calcavecchia, whom I was surprised Stockton had used in foursomes.

109

Although the draw was announced to the press corps, the general public did not hear it until the opening ceremony which was held on the practice ground. The ceremony did go on a bit but I enjoyed it. I do not know about the others but I needed some light entertainment. I had had enough of the team room and the course and the players had probably had enough of me! It was a wonderfully sunny day with, inevitably, that breeze that makes the course play so difficult. The PGA of America had laid on brass and pipe bands and a military display team who did a silent-order routine with their rifles which was remarkably good. I had had the honour of carrying Samuel Ryder's Cup when leading in the European side to the arena and I carefully placed it on a small table on the dais. With the sound of the Atlantic Ocean breaking on the beach behind us, the ceremony got under way. Lord Derby, the president of the PGA, who had been so thrilled to be at Muirfield Village when we won in 1987, was not able to travel with us this time, so Tony Jacklin deputized for him and made a short speech reminding us of the great traditions of the game. Over to the right was another huge stand filled with dignitaries – Deane Beman, the executive director of the US Tour, and his wife were in the group seated there, and right in front were the American team's wives dressed up to the nines in outfits that someone said made them look like ageing chorus girls in a provincial production of *Chorus Line*. That was rather cruel and I would not have been so harsh but they did stand out in the crowd and they were vociferous.

What Samuel Ryder would have made of the proceedings I do not know except that he would probably have been interested to note that, in many respects, the results of the past three matches had turned the tables. We were the quietly confident dominant side. The Americans were the team under pressure, the team for whom winning was now a matter of honour . . . and if recalling and reliving in a sporting context what they considered an American victory in the Gulf War helped to inspire the side, Dave Stockton was quite happy for the public to do so. There was a four-plane fly-past which was over in seconds but the planes were piloted by Gulf War veterans which had many of the American spectators in tears. The Gulf War scenario rankled so much that by the end of the week I would have to say something, but for the moment I bit my lip and could not wait for the real golf to begin.

As I sat there I thought back to previous Ryder Cups, to Eric Brown and to my days as a player when, to be truthful, I did not need a captain to inspire me. Being in the side was inspirational enough. I felt I was there to do, to the best of my ability, what the captain asked. When I was not chosen for a series I just went out and watched the others play, but I always wanted to compete in all the series. Now as captain I was in a different role. The feeling of anticipation was different. My thought now was whether I had done my best for the team in my new situation in which I did not hit a shot. I had no secret yearning to play in the match. Those days were past but deep down I was as keen to do as well in my new role off the course as I had been lucky enough to do on it.

That evening after our family dinner when the players' children had gone off to bed I had a final talk with the side. I had not looked

110

at nor had I had anyone else in the official party run the rule over the Americans in practice because I did not consider that important. I told the team that we had the beating of the Americans but that we could not sit back and expect it to happen. We would have to go out and do the job. Thinking particularly of the rookies who had been given so much help by the more experienced players, especially Seve and Nick, I wanted to emphasize the fact that we could win but not without playing great golf. I have no hesitation in saying they were all terrific. The atmosphere was good. The team spirit, despite all the rumours that flew about Kiawah and which had been started by someone who had no basis for saying so, was excellent. Everyone was happy with the way things had gone and the decisions I had taken. This was a great source of relief to me in what, after all, was a different but equally challenging Ryder Cup role to any I had had in the past. We were all ready to get started. The morning could not come quickly enough.

111

Despair and Delight

When we woke on Friday morning the wind was blowing and we all knew the course would be playing at its toughest. Play had to start early to ensure that we could finish both series and we did, but the eight games – four foursomes in the morning and four four-balls in the afternoon – took all of 10½ hours. The Ryder Cup is an examination of a golfer's skill and nerve but also of his endurance!

'Europe Has It; US Wants It' screamed the banner headlines that morning in the *Charleston Post-Courier* special Ryder Cup pullout section about the 29th match. The consensus of opinion was the Americans might just want to win badly enough to do so but everyone, it seemed, anticipated the match would be a close affair. Even this early – 8 a.m. – red, white and blue were the predominant colours around the clubhouse – Union Jacks from the small group of British supporters were easily spotted, along with the blue flag with its circle of stars representing the 12 Common Market countries, a few Welsh flags held by those there to support Ian Woosnam, and of course Spanish flags which would be waved vigorously over the next three days. The American team had white shirts, red short-sleeved pullovers and navy blue slacks. We were wearing white shirts, brick-red trousers and dark blue sleeveless sweaters.

I double-checked that everyone was fit, made sure that none of the players had any problems and took myself off to the 1st tee to be in position to give each group, as it went off, my best wishes. Sam Torrance joined me as Jose Maria Olazabal and Seve Ballesteros arrived on the tee for their match against Beck and Azinger. There was nothing I needed to say to the Spaniards but 'good luck' – my job was more with the newcomers to Cup golf who might need moral support and encouragement.

So, after two years it was finally happening. Olazabal drove first, right down the middle, but my leading group, whom I had hoped – indeed expected – might make a fast start to encourage the three groups coming behind, found trouble early on. From my position on the tee I could see that although Beck had driven into the waste bunker off the tee Azinger had put his ball on the green while Seve, from the middle of the fairway, went through the green. It needed a delicately played chip back from Olazabal to halve the hole.

At the 2nd Ballesteros hooked his tee shot badly into the marsh and lost the ball. Olazabal, having dropped a second ball, ran out of fairway at the dog-leg and from the difficult sandy lie Seve's attempt to clear a tree that was on his line towards the green failed. In the end the Spaniards took an 8 and Azinger made an eight-footer for a winning birdie 4, and while that was happening the second European pairing were losing the 1st when James and Langer failed to par after Bernhard's approach shot had missed the green. As if that was not bad enough, we lost the 1st hole in the third match as well when the rookies Montgomerie and Gilford, not surprisingly a little nervous, could not match the cast-iron birdie of experienced Irwin who hit his short iron to five feet which the Americans in the crowd – and there were far more of them than European fans scrambling over the sand dunes – considered a tap-in for Lanny Wadkins.

113

Lanny's enthusiasm for the match has remained constant since the first day he teed up in it. That was at Lytham in 1977, the year Nick Faldo made his debut and when Montgomerie was 14 years old and at boarding school in Scotland and Gilford had not yet reached his teens. It was interesting to note that the man the

American captain, Dow Finsterwald, chose to pair him with in the foursomes that year against Brian Barnes and myself was Hale Irwin. They beat us 3 and 1. Of course on this occasion Irwin was deputizing for the injured Pate. Wadkins has that never-say-die attitude notable in his character since he won the 1963 Pee Wee Championship at the age of 13, several years before he attended Wake Forest, Arnold Palmer's alma mater.

Things went rather better in the fourth game in which Nick Faldo and Ian Woosnam halved the 1st with Mark Calcavecchia and Payne Stewart, but not without a struggle. Ian's tee shot had found such a bad spot blocked by a tree growing in the waste bunker on the left that Nick was forced to play short of the green and ended up in more sand. Then Woosie had splashed out to 15 feet. The putt broke slightly right to left and was uphill and Faldo, who had been having such trouble on the greens, holed it. That I hoped would be a lucky omen.

The Ocean course was not one of the easiest on which to move around but I had Manuel Pinero, Angel Gallardo, Tommy Horton (who was also working with BBC Radio who gave as much live coverage on Radio 5 to the match as NBC and BBC Television) and Peter Townsend to keep an eye on how the games were going and how the team members were playing. I knew I would need to put in my fourball pairings for the afternoon an hour before the end of the foursomes, so I needed to know as much as possible about form as the morning wore on. Curiously, the radio wavelength which we had been allocated was an open line which anyone could listen into which meant that I used it sparingly. I never heard Dave speaking on the radio and I suspect he had been allocated a closed channel where he could speak freely without our hearing. I suspected that Dave could hear me, so I kept my comments to fact, checking on positions and passing no comment on how we were doing. I was right to do this because on the final day I wondered aloud how I could watch all 11 singles at the same time . . . and out of the blue he answered that I should know because I had done it before! There had been trouble before with radios in America. In 1987 the American radios all worked perfectly on the hilly Muirfield Village course, but the ones that had been allocated to the Europeans were either not as strong or not as new and certainly did not work.

The opening five holes at Kiawah were as tough, if not tougher, than the closing five and certainly were more than usually demanding in the crosswind. After this opening stretch Ballesteros and Olazabal, who had missed from four feet on the 5th, were two down and remained two down or worse until the 12th.

Mark James had missed an eight-foot birdie putt but par had been good enough to square the second game at the 2nd but the Americans won the short 5th and 6th holes. At the 5th, Couples had hit a glorious 7-iron to four yards on a green where, downwind, it was difficult to stop the ball. Floyd had made the birdie with all the confidence of the polished veteran he is. Langer hooked his tee shot into an impossible lie in the waste bunker at the 6th and, with James having to take a drop, the only hope of the Europeans making a half rested on their opponents three putting. Floyd hit the approach putt from 45 feet and left it 18 inches from the cup.

America were two up in this one and in the third game the rookies were being hit by some of the most impressive golf imaginable in the conditions. At the 3rd, helped by a lucky kick off a tree which deflected Wadkins's ball from going into the sand, Irwin took full advantage, playing one of his glorious irons 180 yards over a tree to six feet. The birdie and the hole were conceded, Montgomerie and Gilford having been in all sorts of trouble. The Europeans, having a rough baptism in Cup competition, could not match another cast-iron birdie at the short 5th where Irwin sank a 10-footer to complement Wadkins's beautifully controlled tee shot. Then, at the par-4 6th, Montgomerie missed an eight-foot putt for par and the rookies had lost another hole. Irwin had splashed out from greenside sand to three feet and Wadkins had sunk the putt to give the US a four-hole lead. Wadkins and Irwin were three under par in far from easy conditions, but it was no consolation to the rookie Europeans or to me that the American couple would have been up on probably any other pairing at that stage with those figures.

Behind in the fourth game Woosnam and Faldo had lost the 2nd and the 4th and were two down as they stepped on to the 6th tee. If Dave Stockton looked rather more perky than me it was hardly surprising but I knew that there was still much golf to be played.

115

But once again – and I cannot explain why it should be – the four-somes were proving a nightmare for us.

Then came the first major incident of the Cup in the top game involving the Spaniards and Azinger and Beck, who had clearly not paid enough care and attention at the lengthy rules meeting. It had to do with ball compression. The Spaniards noticed on the 7th hole – the par 5 which was downwind in contrast to the early holes which had been into the wind – that the Americans had a discussion about which ball to use – the 90-compression or the 100. There was in fact no need for a discussion because although both players were using different compression balls the ball that needed to be used at the 7th was the type Beck had used off the 1st. Seve asked Sam Torrance to contact me but the Spaniards, uncertain whether there had been a breach of the rules or not, did not raise this with the referee until the turn. Before that, Azinger had suggested at the 9th that a referee should be called to tell Seve where to drop after Olazabal had driven well right and off the fairway. The Spaniards made 5 there, lost the hole to the Americans' par and were three down but the ball issue was raised when the players, having been transported the 500 yards to the 10th tee, had a chance to discuss the matter with chief referee Larry Startzel and myself.

At no stage had I worried about who might be playing whom and unlike Dave Stockton I had not tried to pair my men up against the Americans. Neither had I tried to keep players apart as Dave said he tried to do with Azinger and Seve. How he could have done that I shall never know because he had no idea where I was going to place the Spaniards. Dave suspected there was bad feeling between Seve and Paul but Seve said nothing derogatory to me about Azinger and my team had nothing but complete respect for Paul. The peculiar revelations from Stockton several weeks after the match came as a shock because although there had been inci-dents at The Belfry in an earlier singles match between Seve and Paul, this was only the kind of matter that crops up in competition. It is not personal. To be truthful, when the draw came out for the first series and Seve and Olazabal were drawn with Beck and Azinger, I was delighted that our two best players were up against their best.

On that first morning, it became clear to me that if there had been an infringement on the 7th there was nothing we could do about it. If Olazabal and Seve had considered something was wrong they needed to have raised it with the game referee there and then and they had not done so, but the intensity of the situation was such that it rekindled the Azinger-Ballesteros feud from the earlier match. The question was this: Had there been an infringement at the 9th? Azinger said there had not been and pointed out that he and Beck were not cheaters. Seve agreed and pointed out that he had never implied they were. The matter was unable to be resolved either way and I stepped in to end the discussion by telling my pair to play on. The Americans never won another hole as Seve and Ollie turned their three-hole deficit into a 2 and 1 victory.

At the 10th Beck missed from 10 feet and at the 12th Olazabal, who was in brilliant form following his nine-shot runaway success in the now defunct Epson Grand Prix, almost holed his approach. It was Olazabal who squared with a five-foot birdie putt on the 13th and it was his recovery to three feet from the dunes on the left at the 15th that enabled the Spaniards to take the lead when the Americans, now struggling, three putted. It had been Ollie who had played the better of the two but he stepped back to allow Seve to finish off the game 2 and 1 in our favour at the 17th with a 20-foot birdie putt. I was there to congratulate them. Seve told me that he had never at any time considered the match lost but that he and Olazabal, for whom he had nothing but praise, had got off their knees to play well on the back nine.

Sadly it would be the only morning point we would win. James and Langer had lost the 8th to Couples whose reputation as an above-average putter was evident when he sank a 20-footer for a winning birdie. At the 10th James's par putt from 10 feet had slipped past the hole and at four down with eight to play it was always going to be difficult to win this point. Still, I knew that on the back nine, and especially into the left-to-right wind from the 14th, we might have an advantage. I knew Couples, under pressure, had proved suspect at the last Ryder Cup and at the USPGA Championship at Shoal Creek in 1990. We won the 12th, and when he missed from six feet at the 13th to let us win another hole things were looking up. Then Floyd missed the green at the testing short 14th and we were only one down. Now I was hopeful that the first morning's

117

work might not turn out to be so damaging to our chances of retaining the Cup as I had imagined.

Behind, Montgomerie and Gilford had slipped to five down after 11 holes and I could not see that point being salvaged because Irwin and Wadkins were playing too steadily, but Nick and Ian, despite their problems on the greens, had battled back to all-square after making a birdie at the 11th. I wanted to be everywhere at the one time but even as this drama was unfolding I was having to think about the afternoon pairings and their positioning in the draw. Sam Torrance and David Feherty, who had not played in the morning, would be drafted into action; my two top pairings of Seve and Ollie and Ian and Nick would play again; and I decided to put Richardson with James, which meant that I had been unable to place Broadhurst. James had the experience and after the defeat of Montgomerie and Gilford I was loathe to put another all-rookie pairing into action despite the fact that an afternoon gamble with Broadhurst and Richardson might have paid off. That was in my mind as the foursomes progressed and frankly – and this may seem strange to anyone who was there or who watched the match on television – I cannot remember much about what I was doing for part of the time. I was on the course, I was following the games closely, I was being fed information all the time by Manuel and Ken Schofield and I was thinking about the afternoon draw as well. So much was happening so quickly, and fortunes can fluctuate so dramatically in a short space of time, that I had to maintain total concentration. Keeping abreast of the situation in the three matches still going on while considering how best to put out my fourball pairings was as difficult if not more difficult than playing. It was tough for me, but the crowds were loving the golf, especially the Americans.

As I stood on the course looking at one of the scoreboards and hoping it was up-to-date, I could hardly believe that things were going so wrong. When I had seen the draw I had not particularly liked Dave Stockton's pairings and could not imagine why he had Mark Calcavecchia in foursomes when he was, in my opinion, a natural fourball player. I had liked my pairings; I thought I had got them absolutely right. In fact, I would stick with the same pairings again, with Nick and Woosie as the anchor; Seve and Olazabal up front; Bernhard Langer and Mark James second – strong players; and Colin and David Gilford, who on paper should have been a great partnership – both hit the ball so straight and both played so well in practice. I had been sure I was right and could not fathom why things were not working out for me . . . but they were not.

In the second match 49-year-old Floyd, whose putting touch was rock solid, had holed a testing six-footer to prevent Langer and James squaring at the 15th. Both Langer and Floyd were left with eight-footers for par at the next and crucially Floyd holed after Langer had missed. When Fred Couples, showing no signs of cracking and obviously benefiting from Floyd's steadying influence and experience, hit a 3-iron just short of the hole at the short 17th, the match was over. America made the half they needed with par and the points tally was now 1–1. Montgomerie and Gilford, who had missed two chances under pressure just after the turn to reduce their deficit, did take Irwin and Wadkins to the 16th before losing out, but now I needed Woosnam and Faldo to win to tie the series or we went into lunch in the trailer either 2½–1½ or 3–1 down.

We had taken three from the edge of the green at the 12th to lose that, however, and at the 13th Calcavecchia had hit his second shot from 150 yards to five feet and Stewart had holed the little downhill tester to put the United States pair two up again. Then Calcavecchia hit a glorious tee shot to 14 feet at the 219-yards short 14th where Faldo, short off the tee, had nothing but praise for Woosnam's delightfully played pitch that finished close enough to earn a half. The chance of a point had gone when we remained two down with two to play but we won back the dreaded 17th when first Stewart with a 3-iron and then Calcavecchia from the dropping area, hit into the water.

As Dave Stockton and I exchanged team lists for the afternoon fourballs there was still the chance that we might only be a point behind if Woosnam and Faldo could win the last hole, but when Stewart followed up Calcavecchia's booming drive by hitting the green and Woosnam missed the putting surface with his second, the point had been lost.

We were 3–1 down. It was not the start I had planned or hoped for. Looking at the situation positively I hoped that Ian and Nick would be so annoyed at losing and damaging their proud Ryder

119

120

FRIDAY – MORNING FOURSOMES

HOLE	PAR	BALLESTEROS/ OLAZABAL	MATCH POSITION	AZINGER/ BECK	MATCH POSITION
1	4	4	SQ	4	SQ
2	5	8		4	1UP
3	4	4		4	1UP
4	4	6		6	1UP
5	3	4		3	2UP
6	4	4		4	2UP
7	5	5		5	2UP
8	3	3		3	2UP
9	4	5		4	3UP
OUT	36				
10	4	4		5	2UP
11	5	5		5	2UP
12	4	3		4	1UP
13	4	3	SQ	4	SQ
14	3	3	SQ	3	SQ
15	4	4	1UP	5	
16	5	5	1UP	5	
17	3	2	2UP	3	
18	4				
IN	36				
TOTAL	72	MATCH RESULT: BALLESTEROS/OLAZABAL WON (2 & 1)			

HOLE	PAR	LANGER/ JAMES	MATCH POSITION	FLOYD/ COUPLES	MATCH POSITION
1	4	5		4	1UP
2	5	5	SQ	6	SQ
3	4	4	SQ	4	SQ
4	4	5	SQ	5	SQ
5	3	3		2	1UP
6	4	6		4	2UP
7	5	5		5	2UP
8	3	3		2	3UP
9	4	4		4	3UP
OUT	36				
10	4	5		4	4UP
11	5	4		4	4UP
12	4	4		5	3UP
13	4	3		5	2UP
14	3	3		5	1UP
15	4	4		4	1UP
16	5	6		5	2UP
17	3	3		3	2UP
18	4				
IN	36				
TOTAL	72	MATCH RESULT: FLOYD/COUPLES WON (2 & 1)			

HOLE	PAR	GILFORD/ MONTGOMERIE	MATCH POSITION	WADKINS/ IRWIN	MATCH POSITION
1	4	5		3	1UP
2	5	4		4	1UP
3	4	C		W	2UP
4	4	5		5	2UP
5	3	3		2	3UP
6	4	5		4	4UP
7	5	W		C	3UP
8	3	3		2	4UP
9	4	4		4	4UP
OUT	36				
10	4	4		4	4UP
11	5	6		5	5UP
12	4	4		4	5UP
13	4	5		5	5UP
14	3	4		5	4UP
15	4	5		6	3UP
16	5	C		W	4UP
17	3				
18	4				
IN	36				
TOTAL	72	MATCH RESULT: WADKINS/IRWIN WON (4 & 2)			

FRIDAY – MORNING FOURSOMES

HOLE	PAR	FALDO/ WOOSNAM	MATCH POSITION	STEWART/ CALCAVECCHIA	MATCH POSITION
1	4	4	SQ	4	SQ
2	5	5		4	1UP
3	4	4		4	1UP
4	4	C		W	2UP
5	3	4		4	2UP
6	4	4		5	1UP
7	5	5		5	1UP
8	3	3		3	1UP
9	4	4		4	1UP
OUT	36				
10	4	4		4	1UP
11	5	4	SQ	5	SQ
12	4	5		4	1UP
13	4	4		3	2UP
14	3	3		3	2UP
15	4	4		4	2UP
16	5	5		5	2UP
17	3	W		C	1UP
18	4	4		4	1UP
IN	36				
TOTAL	72	MATCH RESULT: STEWART/CALCAVECCHIA WON (1-UP)			

Overall Match Position **Europe 1 US 3**

Cup points record that they would come out and win in the afternoon. I grabbed a sandwich but not the kind that Carmen always makes up specially for Seve and which he has delivered to him at the 10th. Curiously I was not hungry!

Because I wanted to give Seve and Ollie a longish rest at lunchtime, I had put them in the second of the fourball games and, as luck would have it, Stockton put Azinger and Beck in the No. 2 spot as well, so there was an afternoon rematch. If, as he claims, he was trying to keep Azinger and Seve apart, he had failed miserably. James, with his new partner Richardson, faced up to slight, excitable Corey Pavin, the current US top money-earner on his debut at Kiawah, and Calcavecchia in the third game, with Woosnam and Faldo following behind against Couples and Floyd, one of two partnerships Stockton retained. Lanny Wadkins was paired in the opening match of the afternoon with Mark O'Meara against Sam Torrance and David Feherty.

I hoped that there would be no more incidents between Azinger and Beck and the Spaniards although I was aware that Seve seemed to be being blamed for everything in that match, with Azinger even going as far as to suggest that Seve regularly coughed on his (Azinger's) backswing. Paul described Seve quite unjustifiably as the King of Gamesmanship. Such comments are not only untrue but also objectionable and do not do the Cup any good. Seve may have coughed because he had flu all week and was on antibiotics,

121

but not in the way Azinger suggested. I put it all down to the tension that had been built up. The crowds were not as big as expected, which was perhaps just as well because they were having to clamber over the dunes, but they were supportive of all the players. Although the European fans were heavily outnumbered, there were times when it was difficult to judge from long range whether the cheer was for an American win or a European one! Indeed I noticed early on that Seve, Woosie and Nick were as popular with some of the American fans as the members of their own side. Seve was a particular favourite with his tremendous sense of theatre. He is not only a great player, he has the ability, unlike Nick for instance, to react to every shot he plays in a way that ensures all his emotions are there to be seen. Seve does not bottle things up. You are happy or sad depending on his reaction on the course. The ability to carry a crowd like a great actor carries an audience is something that has always given him extra special appeal.

I knew we needed to hit back quickly to ensure that the momentum which had gone the Americans way in the morning would not be allowed to continue and James and Richardson made just the start the team and I were looking for. James birdied the 2nd and 3rd holes from 20 and 15 feet against Pavin and Calcavecchia. We were quickly two up and big Steven got in the act when he used his distinctive putting style to cut in a 20-footer for a winning birdie at the 6th. Then he holed a bunker shot at the 7th for an eagle. We were four up after seven and it was only then that I realized just how much Steven was enjoying the occasion, the pressure, the challenge. He had taken to the Ryder Cup like a duck to water. Pavin, who won the German Open in 1983, birdied the 8th and the Americans won the 9th with a par but my pairing was working well. At the 11th, the 576-yarder which runs along the swamp side of the course, Richardson – who had taken his mother, his father, who is pro at the Lee-on-the-Solent club, his three sisters and his girlfriend Helen to Kiawah as a treat – demonstrated his awesome (if I may borrow a word from Dave Stockton's vocabulary that week) power with a drive and 230-yard long iron to within 12 feet of the hole. We won 5 and 4. It was a tremendous filip.

Behind them, Woosnam and Faldo were again in trouble. They were not playing their best golf and not combining as well as Floyd and Couples. They were badly out of sorts on the greens again, especially after the turn, and although I felt that both were experienced enough to lift themselves to win, it did not work out on the first day. We were never up but still all-square after nine holes and it was anybody's game. At the 10th, from a horrid lie, Floyd hit a magnificent shot to 15 feet and was the only one of the four to make a birdie, but the most important hole of the afternoon round was undoubtedly the long 11th which we looked like winning but lost. Woosie had an eagle chance from just off the green pin-high on the left down the slope. He sent it three feet past and missed the return. Floyd was lying five feet away in three and Faldo, assuming Ian would look after things, had not bothered to play his fourth shot from through the green in the scrubby sand. In the end Floyd holed to win the hole with a birdie. Couples coaxed one in on the next for another winning birdie and hit a 153-yard second shot to four feet to win a third hole in a row. Woosie missed from 15 feet and Faldo from nine feet for a half. At that moment I made my mind up to split the partnership on the second day. Floyd rolled in a 20-footer for a half at the short 14th. Minutes later it was all over. It was a surprisingly heavy defeat for us – and our only afternoon reversal.

I was at the 15th when the match ended and drove back the mile or so to the trailer with two very disappointed and downhearted superstars. Nick said nothing, but it was easy to appreciate what the world No. 3 was feeling. Ian, typically, was more forthcoming and felt totally responsible. He said he felt bad on the greens and did not want to play the next day. I told him we would talk about it later.

The score was now 4–2, but Seve and Olazabal completed the double over Azinger and Beck this time without incident and again by 2 and 1. It was always a tight game with the US pair twice up early on but with the Spaniards taking the lead after Seve won the short 8th with a birdie. Olazabal was again playing superbly and Seve was dove-tailing beautifully but it was back to all-square after 13 holes when the Spaniards made their final push, cheered on by the Europeans and particularly by one fan from Barcelona who carried a huge Spanish flag and waved it to signal hole victories. Seve hit his tee shot to eight feet at the 14th to go one up and won the match when both Azinger and Beck went into the water to lose the 17th after he had put the pressure on by hitting the green.

I was aware that I was seeing very little of Dave Stockton on the course. We seemed to be going our own ways. He was always with his main pairings. I was not. I left the stars alone and went with the others. We seldom met up and if we had that first afternoon he would have had the most worried look. His men were faltering. We were hitting back well and I could not have been more delighted.

It was turning out to be a better afternoon than morning and it improved even more when Feherty and Torrance, three down after 10 holes to Mark O'Meara and Wadkins, fought back to get a half. The partnership I had always planned on using at Kiawah was not letting me down. David Feherty holed a 25-foot pitch shot to win the 11th but in golf it is swings and roundabouts and he missed two difficult birdie chances on the run in that would have squared matters with two to play.

We were still one down but we had the honour at the 17th and Sam hit a corker to two feet. Amazingly, Wadkins and O'Meara both hit to five feet and O'Meara made the half. Down the last it was rookie Feherty who was left with the putt to end all-square. The length was eight feet and the hole must have looked incredibly small but the ball disappeared and we were back in the game. We had taken the afternoon fourball series 2$\frac{1}{2}$–1$\frac{1}{2}$. After the first day there was just a point in it with the Americans leading 4$\frac{1}{2}$–3$\frac{1}{2}$ and I had every hope that, having grabbed the initiative, we could follow that up the next day with a foursomes performance of which we could be proud.

I felt that it would be best to rest Nick and Ian for one of the following day's series with a view to getting points from them in the singles. My theory was that Nick's game was still so good through the green that even putting badly he could do well in foursomes and I reckoned that David Gilford, who had been going so well in practice, was the man to play with him. I remembered Bernhard Langer had played four times with Nick in fourballs and foursomes and won three of those matches but, at the time, I reckoned that Gilford, who seldom misses a shot and is very consistent, would be perfect for Nick. This way I could give Paul Broadhurst, who had admitted to me that he was not a great foursomes player, his first

124

FRIDAY – AFTERNOON FOURBALLS

HOLE	PAR	TORRANCE	FEHERTY	MATCH POSITION	WADKINS	O'MEARA	MATCH POSITION
1	4	4	4	SQ		4	SQ
2	5		6		4		1UP
3	4	4	4		4	4	1UP
4	4	4	4		4	4	1UP
5	3	3	4		3	3	1UP
6	4	4	4		4	4	1UP
7	5	4	4		5	4	1UP
8	3	4	4		3	3	2UP
9	4	4	5		3	3	3UP
OUT	36						
10	4	4	4		4	4	3UP
11	5	4	4		5	5	2UP
12	4	4	5		4	4	2UP
13	4	4	5		4	4	2UP
14	3	4	2		3	3	1UP
15	4	4	4		4	4	1UP
16	5	5	5		5	5	1UP
17	3	2	3		3	2	1UP
18	4	5	4	SQ	5	5	SQ
IN	36						
TOTAL	72	MATCH RESULT: (HALVED)					

HOLE	PAR	BALLESTEROS	OLAZABAL	MATCH POSITION	AZINGER	BECK	MATCH POSITION
1	4	4	5	SQ	4	4	SQ
2	5	6	5	SQ		5	SQ
3	4	4	4		3	4	1UP
4	4	4	4		4	4	1UP
5	3	3	2	SQ	3	3	SQ
6	4	4	4		3	4	1UP
7	5	4	5	SQ	5	5	SQ
8	3	2	3	1UP	3	3	
9	4	5	4	1UP	4	5	
OUT	36						
10	4	4	3	1UP	3	4	
11	5	5	4	1UP	4	5	
12	4	5	4	1UP		4	
13	4		4	SQ	3	4	SQ
14	3	2	3	1UP	3	3	
15	4	4	4	1UP	4	4	
16	5	5	4	1UP	4	4	
17	3	3		2UP	5		
18	4						
IN	36						
TOTAL	72	MATCH RESULT: BALLESTEROS/OLAZABAL WON (2 & 1)					

HOLE	PAR	RICHARDSON	JAMES	MATCH POSITION	PAVIN	CALCAVECCHIA	MATCH POSITION
1	4	4	4	SQ	4	4	SQ
2	5		4	1UP	5		
3	4	5	3	2UP	4	5	
4	4	4	4	2UP	4	4	
5	3		3	2UP	3	3	
6	4	3		3UP	4	4	
7	5	3		4UP		4	
8	3	3	3	3UP	2		
9	4	5	5	2UP	4	4	
OUT	36						
10	4	4	4	2UP	4	4	
11	5	4	5	3UP	5	5	
12	4	4		4UP	5		
13	4	4	4	4UP	4	4	
14	3	4	3	5UP	4	4	
15	4						
16	5						
17	3						
18	4						
IN	36						
TOTAL	72	MATCH RESULT: RICHARDSON/JAMES WON (5 & 4)					

125

HOLE	PAR	FALDO	WOOSNAM	MATCH POSITION	FLOYD	COUPLES	MATCH POSITION
1	4	4	4		5	3	1UP
2	5	6	6		5	5	2UP
3	4	4	3		4	4	1UP
4	4	4	3	SQ	4	4	SQ
5	3	3	3	SQ	3	4	SQ
6	4	4	4		3	4	1UP
7	5	4	5		5	4	1UP
8	3	2	3	SQ	3	3	SQ
9	4	4	4	SQ	4	4	SQ
OUT	36						
10	4	4	4		3	4	1UP
11	5	5	5		4	5	2UP
12	4	4	4		4	3	3UP
13	4	4	4		5	3	4UP
14	3	3	3		3	4	4UP
15	4	4	4		4	3	5UP
16	5						
17	3						
18	4						
IN	36						
TOTAL	72	MATCH RESULT: FLOYD/COUPLES WON (5 & 3)					

Europe 2½ US 1½
Overall Match Position **Europe 4½ US 3½**

game in the afternoon fourballs. Woosie, who had reconsidered his position and was now willing to play if required on the second day, still reckoned he would be bad news for his partner in foursomes, so I rested him and told him that he and Paul Broadhurst would play together in the Saturday afternoon fourballs as lead couple. I wanted someone good to play with Broadhurst in his first match and Woosnam seemed to be the man. Clearly I would keep Ballesteros and Olazabal, our only first-day foursomes winners. Feherty and Torrance had earned the right to continue, as had James and Richardson. Woosnam, Langer, Montgomerie and Broadhurst would sit out the third series.

Play had begun at 8.0 a.m. and had gone on into the gloaming at 6.30 p.m. but it had been riveting golf. One local newspaperman described it as a human endurance test. I knew it had been a tough day for my team and Dave Stockton described it as 'brutal' for everyone. His injured team man Steve Pate had walked the course but would not be ready for foursomes play the following day.

We met for a drink and dinner in the apartment and we had our usual team meeting to assess the day's play and to allow me to confirm the next day's foursomes pairings. I wrestled in my own mind about having put the two rookies, who had played well in practice, in at the deep end. Had I been unfair to them, or was it just that they had come up against an American couple who, on the day and in the conditions, were simply devastating? Should I have played each of them with a more experienced man? Had I been wrong not to have secured a spot for in-form Paul Broadhurst before the second afternoon's fourballs? What mistakes had I made, how many more would I make or was I being too hard on myself? With hindsight it was easy to see where I might have gone wrong, but the captain does not have the advantage of hindsight and I had had to take the decisions on the hoof, as it were. The strains and stresses of the day and the anticipation of more gruelling but glorious golf to come meant most of my team had a very early night, but I slept fitfully.

9

Fighting Back

The wind on the Saturday was still blowing towards the ocean which meant that the last five holes were again going to be playing particularly tough. The greenkeeping staff of around 150, some drawn from the other courses on the island, were up again before first light to make sure the Ocean course was at its best. Because of the wind factor the pin positions for the day were double-checked and the holes not cut until about an hour before the play began. No one wanted the course to be unplayable, even by the best golfers in the world, but the PGA of America did not exactly make it easy for them with some very tight second-day positions.

Although I had kept Seve and Ollie together, Dave had not retained his twice-beaten Beck and Azinger partnership. He replaced Beck with Mark O'Meara and they were playing third against Faldo and Gilford. In the top game the buoyant Feherty and Torrance had the task of trying to hold first-day foursomes winners Lanny Wadkins and Hale Irwin, the partnership Stockton much admired. He kept together Payne Stewart and Mark Calcavecchia and they faced up to James and Richardson, with the unbeaten Spaniards having to tackle the unbeaten Floyd and

Couples at the bottom of the draw. There are no easy games in the Ryder Cup. I knew that from my experience. The pressure of playing for your country and for a team instead of for yourself is considerable, but I was not disheartened as I saw the players off in the early morning light, the wind whipping into their faces as it blew over the salt marshes towards the Atlantic.

I knew that as far as Dave and I were concerned I was less visible than he was on the course and less talkative than him at the press conferences but I knew, too, that all my team members were experienced enough competitors and well enough aware of what they had to do not to need me spending my time dashing frantically from game to game. They knew I was there and watching and that, if they needed anything on the course, I would see they got it. I made a point of joining every match at some stage, giving quiet encouragement, but my whole strategy was to try and reduce the tremendous hype that had enveloped Kiawah. Because of the design of the course I watched more on the front nine than the back. I just attached myself to a match and followed it for a few holes. Indeed at one point after I had walked two or three holes with Seve and Olazabal, Seve asked me why I was with them. I answered because I was enjoying watching them play, as were the thousands of spectators! They were hugely experienced in the supercharged atmosphere. I knew how tough it was to concentrate and had been proud of the way the team had gone about their business on the first day when it was clear the American players were whipping up the crowds. That encouragement of the fans to react vociferously would, I knew, get worse as the match progressed, but I was sure we could cope.

In the press tent I had given no real indication of my thinking, fearing that it might give Dave a clue as to how I might distribute my pairings in future series or how I might deploy my men in the singles. I played it quite close to the chest, answering the questions in a straightforward manner without embellishing them in any way, like Tony had done in the past or Dave was doing this time. The day before I had been quizzed about placing the Spaniards second instead of first in the fourballs. The answer was simple. I wanted to give them as long between their foursomes and fourball matches as I could, within reason, but I had not said this as it would have given Dave a clue about my plans. I was learning all the time. I may have worked with Tony and watched him in action at close quarters in the matches since 1985 – and that undoubtedly helped – but being captain, having the ultimate responsibility, takes some getting used to.

Quite naturally I cared for and worried about and sometimes sympathized with the team members, who knew I knew how they felt because I had been through it all as a player myself. I tried to give each of them my total support throughout the three days and every one of them supported me, each doing exactly as I asked. Yet on the second day I quickly realized that my gamble on putting the reliable David Gilford with Nick Faldo in the hope of earning a foursomes point was not working. I watched them over the first few holes when they went two down but had no reason to suspect they would crash to a record-equalling 7 and 6 defeat. They just did not click the way I hoped they would.

While Faldo was having his frustrating problems on the greens, and Gilford too, O'Meara and Azinger were not. O'Meara rolled in a 20-footer for a winning birdie at the 1st and Gilford, short in two with his approach to the elevated green, missed a shortish putt for par to let the Americans win the 3rd. Azinger holed an eight-foot birdie at the 5th and Faldo, the frustration getting to him, missed from six feet to lose the 6th. Azinger, the man Nick beat to win the Open Championship in the mists of Muirfield in 1987, fired a 2-iron 220 yards into the heart of the green for an eagle chance at the 7th but Gilford was short. Faldo did not make a good job of the next shot from a bare lie and amazingly we were five down after seven holes.

I saw little of this as I concentrated on other games but the end for them was not long in coming. Although Faldo played a tremendous one-handed backwards shot from the rough to earn him and Gilford a half at the 11th, they were by now six down and their sad, untypical morning performance ended when Nick hit into the water at the 12th. Perfectionist Nick, dreadfully upset and angry with his own performance, had, I was told, come over badly on television, giving the impression he was doing little to help Gilford. I spoke with David afterwards and he said there had been no trouble between him and Nick who had been very supportive in a match that just went wrong from the start. Criticism of Nick, he said, was very unfair.

Nick knew he would not be playing in the afternoon because I had told him that the night before, so there was no question of my having to change my plans and drop him for the afternoon four-balls. He wanted to be a huge success for our side and the frustration of not being able to finish off his good play through the green with sound putting was eating him up. We all knew the way Nick can play and we all wanted to help him, but there was nothing we could do to get the putts to drop. Only he could solve that problem and he would spend the afternoon trying to do just that with coach Leadbetter on the 1st green after the last of the fourballs had gone through. He is a loner and, like all Cancerians, does from time to time disappear into his protective shell but his only thought was to sort out his putting so that he could win a singles point on the last day to avoid the embarrassment of a personal white-wash.

As the hot sun beat down for the second day running and the breeze added to the problems of sunburn and chapped lips, Seve and Olazabal were in invincible form, going through the turn three up in their match with Floyd and Couples. I noticed that Dave Renwick, Olazabal's caddie, who was not wearing a hat, was getting badly burned. The Spanish partnership was working so well I did not want anything to upset them and I did not want Dave, who has been with Olazabal for five years, to be unable to work on the next day. I gave him my white Panama. It was better that I was burned a bit, rather than him!

We had lost one game, were up in one, but down in the two others. For the second morning running the foursomes play was taking its toll. I cannot understand why we do not play foursomes well, a problem that is shared with the Walker Cup players from our side of the Atlantic. Maybe it is something in our character, but it does seem strange that the same players, using their own ball, can be so much more effective than when sharing a ball with a partner. It is something that needs to be examined and corrected because it is daft to give the Americans a start every time.

Sam and David had been up twice on the front nine but by the 10th it was Wadkins and Irwin who had the edge. At the 11th it looked as if we would square matters but sadly we did not and it would prove a crucial hole. Wadkins was in the waste area off the tee and Irwin failed to clear the sea oats completely in two shots. Torrance's drive was perfect and Feherty, aware that the Americans were in trouble and unlikely to make par, might have been better advised to play up safely short of the green rather than have a go at it 280 yards away in the distance. He was confident, however, he would leave Sam putting for an eagle. Instead the ball ended up in a deep waste bunker. In fact the Americans took 6 but so did we. After Sam blasted out through the green, David hit the fourth shot 10 feet past the cup and Sam missed. The Americans won the 12th with par after Torrance gambled and went for the flag at an awkward spot back right and ended up in the swamp. Although Sam coaxed a 45-footer up the hill to within an inch or two of the hole to win back the 13th, we lost the next three played into the teeth of the wind. Sam missed a three-footer at the 14th, David a five-footer at the next, and minutes later we were beaten 4 and 2 when we took five to get on the green.

Now the question was: could James and Richardson make it 2–2? If they lost to Stewart and Calcavecchia we would be conceding the foursomes 3–1 for the second day running. We had been up early on in this game but were two down after 10 having lost the 9th to Stewart's 15-foot birdie and the 10th, where James had driven into trouble and Steve had missed a 15-footer for par. Try as hard as they could the European pair just could not chip away at the Americans' lead on the most difficult day yet. Again I hoped that when turning into the closing five holes we might have the edge but with two to play James, competing in his fifth Cup match, and Richardson, on his debut, were still two down, James having missed a five-foot putt in the blustery wind that would have won us the 16th. The best they could do was square the match – and half points are, of course, just as important when it comes to the end result. When Stewart failed to carry the lagoon at the short 17th, we won back that hole. Now we needed to win the last.

I had already indicated my afternoon fourball pairings – Ian Woosnam would be back with Paul Broadhurst to lead the way, Langer would return to partner Montgomerie, Seve and Ollie would play last and I had decided that James and Richardson were getting on so well that they should be retained for a third time. They would play third in the afternoon but, for the moment, my mind was on the final, vital foursomes and whether the Spaniards would manage to hold on to their unbeaten record. All the fans were now following this last game and they saw James's drive end up in the sand. Calcavecchia hit the fairway but Stewart ended up short of the green, as did Richardson from a not-too-clever lie. When Calcavecchia chipped to 10 feet and James to four, it looked as if we were going to get the half point, but after Stewart had missed for par, so too did Richardson. It was disappointing for us but even more so for him. He had played well but at the end, watched by millions around the world on television and hundreds round the green, he must have felt he had let the side down.

As Stewart and Calcavecchia celebrated their escape – they had finished bogey, triple-bogey, bogey, yet lost only one hole – I consoled Richardson and told him that he and James would be in action again shortly. Far from being despondent, James was annoyed and angry with himself and he did not allow Richardson to dwell on the situation. He was not the first player, nor would he be the last, to miss a putt that he would normally hole with ease. This was the Ryder Cup, and his first one. Spurred on by James, they had a quick lunch and were delighted to have the chance to make amends in the fourballs.

Although Dave Stockton had not chosen the USPGA champion John Daly to play in the Ryder Cup, Daly clearly did not bear any grudges. He had declined Stockton's invitation to come along as a spectator and soak up the atmosphere but he did contact the US captain to wish the team all the best. In more descriptive language he had faxed: 'Good Luck and Kick Butt'. Our butts certainly had been kicked in the foursomes because we had won only two of them and both times the Spaniards had been responsible. I might have been a bit depressed by the situation if there had not been so much else going on. Anyway, I have never given up as a player and was not prepared to give the Americans any indication of my concern for our position at this stage in the match. We had clawed our way back on the first day with a good performance in the foursomes and there was no reason why we should not do the same again on the

133

SARURDAY – MORNING FOURSOMES

HOLE	PAR	FEHERTY/ TORRANCE	MATCH POSITION	WADKINS/ IRWIN	MATCH POSITION
1	4	4	1UP	6	
2	5	6	SQ	5	SQ
3	4	4	1UP	5	
4	4	4	1UP	4	
5	3	3	1UP	3	
6	4	5	SQ	4	SQ
7	5	4	SQ	4	SQ
8	3	4		3	1UP
9	4	4	SQ	5	SQ
OUT	36				
10	4	4		3	1UP
11	5	6		6	1UP
12	4	5		4	2UP
13	4	4		5	1UP
14	3	5		4	2UP
15	4	5		4	3UP
16	5	C		W	4UP
17	3				
18	4				
IN	36				
TOTAL	72	MATCH RESULT: WADKINS/IRWIN WON (4 & 2)			

SARURDAY – MORNING FOURSOMES

HOLE	PAR	JAMES/ RICHARDSON	MATCH POSITION	CALCAVECCHIA/ STEWART	MATCH POSITION
1	4	4	1UP	5	
2	5	6	SQ	5	SQ
3	4	5		4	1UP
4	4	4		4	1UP
5	3	3	SQ	4	SQ
6	4	4	SQ	4	SQ
7	5	4	1UP	5	
8	3	3	SQ	2	SQ
9	4	4		3	1UP
OUT	36				
10	4	5		4	2UP
11	5	5		6	1UP
12	4	5		3	2UP
13	4	4		4	2UP
14	3	3		3	2UP
15	4	4		4	2UP
16	5	6		6	2UP
17	3	W		C	1UP
18	4	5		5	1UP
IN	36				
TOTAL	72	MATCH RESULT: CALCAVECCHIA/STEWART WON (1-UP)			

SARURDAY – MORNING FOURSOMES

HOLE	PAR	FALDO/ GILFORD	MATCH POSITION	AZINGER/ O'MEARA	MATCH POSITION
1	4	5		3	1UP
2	5	5		5	1UP
3	4	5		4	2UP
4	4	5		5	2UP
5	3	3		2	3UP
6	4	5		4	4UP
7	5	C		W	5UP
8	3	3		3	5UP
9	4	5		5	5UP
OUT	36				
10	4	4		3	6UP
11	5	5		5	6UP
12	4	C		W	7UP
13	4				
14	3				
15	4				
16	5				
17	3				
18	4				
IN	36				
TOTAL	72	MATCH RESULT: AZINGER/O'MEARA WON (7 & 6)			

SARURDAY – MORNING FOURSOMES

HOLE	PAR	BALLESTEROS/ OLAZABAL	MATCH POSITION	FLOYD/ COUPLES	MATCH POSITION
1	4	5		4	1UP
2	5	5		5	1UP
3	4	4	SQ	5	SQ
4	4	4	SQ	4	SQ
5	3	2	1UP	3	
6	4	4	2UP	5	
7	5	4	2UP	4	
8	3	3	2UP	3	
9	4	4	3UP	5	
OUT	36				
10	4	4	3UP	4	
11	5	5	3UP	5	
12	4	4	3UP	4	
13	4	4	3UP	4	
14	3	3	4UP	4	
15	4	5	3UP	4	
16	5	6	3UP	6	
17	3				
18	4				
IN	36				
TOTAL	72	MATCH RESULT: BALLESTEROS/OLAZABAL WON (3 & 2)			

Europe 1 US 3
Overall Match Position **Europe 4½ US 7½**

second afternoon with the help of our loyal support, not least the wives.

In the old days no one would have been asked whether he wanted to take his wife to a Ryder Cup match, but things have changed and now the wives are an integral part of the official party. Indeed, all the wives were presented with outfits which complemented the colours worn by the players on the days of the match – and these I may say were far more subdued than the clothes worn by the gung-ho American wives. The team really appreciated the role the wives played. In a more general sense, Jane James and Sam Torrance's Suzanne are really lively and good at keeping spirits up on and off the course. At all times throughout the three days they were on the course helping the team, encouraging them.

Having regained the initiative at the end of the first day we had lost it once more and those comments about disharmony in our camp were resurfacing. I got to hear of it on the course when listening to the television coverage in my ear-piece. I was so upset for the team when commentator Ben Wright came out with all this disinformation. I will never know how it started but I do know it was only talked about when things were going badly for us in the foursomes. There was no talk of a so-called rift when we were doing well in fourball games. I admit that some of the players looked unhappy, but only because they were unhappy with their games.

Our team spirit was still good and we proved this when we came out and won the second series of fourballs 3½–½. It was a tremendous afternoon of high drama for us in which we dragged ourselves back into the match brilliantly – hardly the performance of a team that was being ripped apart by internal disputes. I am still fuming at the implication which was so wrong and so damaging. Fortunately the team had enough on their plates and either ignored what they heard about our apparent disunity or just did not hear about it all. I should add that Ben Wright had infuriated me earlier by rehashing the erroneous reactions to my *Sunday Mirror* piece during the Open – about the Europeans doing well at Birkdale – and had even tried to provoke Lanny Wadkins into commenting about it, but the match by now had reached a critical stage. I had more important things on my mind.

The atmosphere on the course was electric. The American fans were sensing victory but our European supporters were unwilling to concede an inch and were determined to cheer us on to a second fourball success. There seemed to be people on every sand dune wishing us well and clearly enjoying an event which the PGA of America will never need to 'hard sell' again. The impact of the 21 hours of live television around the world was considerable, too, even if the wind made on-course communications somewhat tricky for John Shrewsbury and the BBC team. What was curious, however, was that no television station in Australia thought the Cup worth taking, although the Australians support us so strongly against the Americans and the fans down under are among the most enthusiastic. Sometimes I bumped into the radio men – Julian Tutt, George Bayley who lost his voice, Alan Green, released for one week from his north of England football beat, and, of course, one of my own righthand men, Tommy Horton. Rob Bonnett was there from BBC 'Breakfast Time', too, although he, like the journalists, did most of his interviewing after play was over. In fact it was fairly crowded on the course with the players, the caddies, the referees, the official observers, the radio men and the television personnel with their directional gun mikes that sometimes pick up conversations and words best left unheard! Yet it is all part of the Cup match now.

The media tent this year was the biggest ever and, because of the problem of course access, the PGA had installed television sets at every third seat for the press covering the event. We had considerable support from the European press corps and my request that the players not be hassled during the matches was never challenged, even if there were times when I knew an extra quote or a quiet little exclusive interview would have been helpful. I, too, was being treated gently in the press interviews. The journalists from this side of the Atlantic were as keen as I was for us to hold on to the Cup – to the extent, I am told, that the cheers on the course were sometimes echoed in the tent, initially by the European contingent and later in the week by the Americans. Partisanship was everywhere.

On that second afternoon, Woosnam and Broadhurst, who was aching to get started, were up against Azinger and evergreen Irwin. I felt that Langer and Montgomerie would have the edge on Pavin and Steve Pate, drafted in for the first time despite his badly bruised side. James and Richardson faced up to Wadkins and Wayne Levi, who until now had not been used, and Seve and Olazabal were in against Couples again, partnered by Payne Stewart rather than Floyd, who was being rested for the singles. So Dave and I had ensured that all our team members had played before the singles came along, something I had always promised.

137

What delighted me particularly on that second afternoon was the way that Woosnam, asked to go out and do a job, rallied round so effectively as the perfect partner for 26-year-old Broadhurst, who played so well on his debut. It was always a tight game against Azinger and Irwin with never more than a hole in it until we won on the 17th, a great hole for spectators. The dunes behind the green were always packed with people and anyone who made a point of being there to see everyone through on the first two days got value for money in terms of excitement and drama.

It was a tough day and not too many holes were going to be won with birdies, but Paul nearly holed from a bunker at the short 8th. His ball hit the pin and stayed out, but the Americans took 4 to lose the hole and the game was all-square. The Americans quickly regained the advantage at the 9th which curves back round towards the clubhouse area, when Azinger, who was playing as if inspired, finished off a superb approach shot of 150 yards by sinking the five-footer for a birdie. Broadhurst may have waited for his call to action but when it came he, like the others, was ready with his red-hot short game. At the 10th he rolled in a 30-footer with such calm control that you might have been forgiven for thinking the Midlander had been playing in Ryder Cup matches for years. At the 13th he sank a 10-footer to put us up for the first time, but the climax came at the 17th with the match board still showing Europe one up. All four players missed the green – Irwin fading the ball into the water on the wind that hardly suited his natural left-to-right game. Azinger could not make 3, but Woosnam, showing the expertise that won him the Masters and the New Orleans, the Monte Carlo and the Mediterranean Opens, splashed out of a most awkward lie in the sand to three feet and holed for 3 to make sure of the point. At the death Woosie had played a glorious winner and the partnership had worked. Woosnam had been the right man to inspire Broadhurst and, in turn, the rookie had played his not inconsiderable part in the rehabilitation of his more experienced partner. Maybe Ian was still not all that comfortable with his putting, but the win was the boost his confidence needed for the singles still to come, remembering he had played four and lost four in previous matches.

138

Behind them another rookie, Colin Montgomerie, was partnering Bernhard Langer to a point with a five-hour match against Pavin and Pate. This partnership had also clicked. I was getting it right! We won 2 and 1 and were never down in the game in which Pate gave us a glimpse of his badly bruised abdomen when getting treatment and a rub-down from Brett Fischer, the US team's physio, on the 9th tee. He had sunk a par-saving putt at the 8th and then one at the 9th to win that hole and take the match into Kiawah's tough back nine all-square. If the bruising hurt a lot he was still able to hit powerful drives without grimacing although the injury was, he told the physio, 'tightening up'. Two mistakes by the Americans allowed the Europeans to go two up, but then Langer, usually emotionless on the course, had cause to thank Montgomerie. Pavin, not quite so exuberant as he would prove to be on the last day when the situation overwhelmed him, hit the flag at the 13th with a 100-yard approach shot. Montgomerie hit to three feet from similar range and holed for a half, then crucially at the 15th holed one of those testing downhill 18-footers for the half after Pate had putted in from off the green. The disappointment of the first day's four-somes had been forgotten. Two holes later the point was in the European bag and our spectators' cheers were being heard above the American whoops and hollers.

The excitement was intense on the course as those players who had won fell back to support their colleagues still in action in the games behind. The wives were there, too, encouraging their husbands or any European team man. The noise from the supporters of both sides drowned out the ocean breakers and the sea birds' calls. We had all forgotten, too, about the alligators in the swampland and the rattlesnakes in the dunes. We were all too focused on what was happening on the course and, from a European point of view, it was excellent viewing with James and Richardson, who had won the first three holes, two of them with Richardson birdies, holding a three-up lead after the 15th. They could not be beaten. Steve is one of the longest hitters I have seen and in Mark James he had the perfect partner. James, when I chose him as my final wild card, had promised not to let me down and he was true to his word. Although we lost the 16th, where Richardson was in the water off the tee and Wadkins, battler that he is, hit a 200-yard second shot to two feet, we clinched victory – again at the 17th.

Now we were level at 7½ points each and we had the chance to take the lead into the singles if the Spaniards could continue their brilliant winning streak. The golf that I had watched had been remarkable. The Ocean course at Kiawah was not easy, quite impossible I would imagine, even off the forward trees, for resort golfers when the wind is even just a light zephyr, but the members of both teams were hitting masses of not only good but great shots in the strong breeze. The scoring was higher than usual and several of the team had indicated they would have been hating every minute of it, had they been involved in card-and-pencil play, because of the scores they would have been putting down on the card. But this was matchplay. How many did not matter as long as it was one stroke less than the opposition and the hole was won. The match these days is one of the most draining physically and mentally in sport. There is no let-up. One slip and a hole is lost, a game point squandered. I felt the tension too. It hurt me when one of the team

139

hit a less than perfect shot or swung in other than the best way. However, the standard of play was incredible – something the fans appreciated. No longer do we need to be apologetic about European golf – it was fabulous to watch and I was proud of the team.

The drama built up as the players battled to finish before the light faded completely. Couples and Stewart, who had been down in the early part of the match, were now two up with six to play. Seve had praised Olazabal for the quality of his play in earlier rounds but it was he who sank the 10-foot winning birdie putt on the 13th and another of similar length at the 15th where it dropped in through the back door to level matters. Couples had to hole from five feet for a half at the short 17th, where Olazabal had missed his six-foot chance to win the hole after another glorious tee shot. As I stood watching I felt for him. His tee shot had deserved better.

We now needed to make sure that we won or at worst halved the last. Winning the 18th would be nice because it would complete the whitewash, something Seve was well aware of despite the fact that the scoreboards were few and far between and well below the standard of on-course information we set over here. The huge crowds streamed down the last as, out to sea, the lights of the shrimp boats were now clearly visible in the dusk. It was getting dark. It reminded me of the time Nick Faldo beat Scott Hoch in the Masters when it would have been impossible for them to have continued the play-off as darkness fell. It would not have been practical to play any extra holes at Kiawah but of course Ryder Cup tradition is that matches all-square after 18 holes are halved. With Seve having driven his tee shot into a pot bunker and Calcavecchia out of it as well, the result depended on Olazabal holing from six feet and Stewart from half that distance for a half. They both duly did and after two days the score was all tied up. Whichever team won the singles would pick up the Cup. The spectators, again well satisfied, headed back either to their villas or the Kiawah Island Inn on the island, or to nearby Seabrook Island or Charleston, for a bath and dinner.

In the press tent the story of the day was being filed to cities all over the world by journalists using lap-top computers. Gordon Turnbull was supervising BBC Radio's midnight newsroom sports-

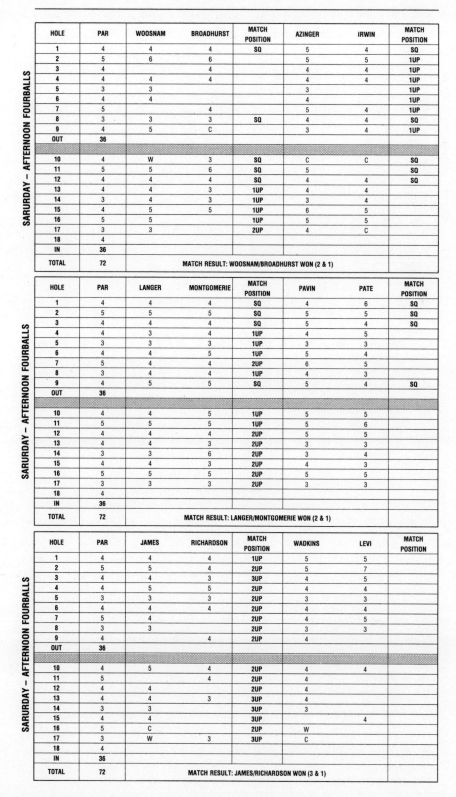

SARURDAY – AFTERNOON FOURBALLS

HOLE	PAR	WOOSNAM	BROADHURST	MATCH POSITION	AZINGER	IRWIN	MATCH POSITION
1	4	4	4	SQ	5	4	SQ
2	5	6	6		5	5	1UP
3	4		4		4	4	1UP
4	4	4	4		4	4	1UP
5	3	3			3		1UP
6	4	4			4		1UP
7	5		4		5	4	1UP
8	3	3	3	SQ	4	4	SQ
9	4	5	C		3	4	1UP
OUT	36						
10	4	W	3	SQ	C	C	SQ
11	5	5	6	SQ	5		SQ
12	4	4	4	SQ	4	4	SQ
13	4	4	3	1UP	4	4	
14	3	4	3	1UP	3	4	
15	4	5	5	1UP	6	5	
16	5	5		1UP	5	5	
17	3	3		2UP	4	C	
18	4						
IN	36						
TOTAL	72	MATCH RESULT: WOOSNAM/BROADHURST WON (2 & 1)					

SARURDAY – AFTERNOON FOURBALLS

HOLE	PAR	LANGER	MONTGOMERIE	MATCH POSITION	PAVIN	PATE	MATCH POSITION
1	4	4	4	SQ	4	6	SQ
2	5	5	5	SQ	5	5	SQ
3	4	4	4	SQ	5	4	SQ
4	4	3	4	1UP	4	5	
5	3	3	3	1UP	3	3	
6	4	4	5	1UP	5	4	
7	5	4	4	2UP	6	5	
8	3	4	4	1UP	4	3	
9	4	5	5	SQ	5	4	SQ
OUT	36						
10	4	4	5	1UP	5	5	
11	5	5	5	1UP	5	6	
12	4	4	4	2UP	5	5	
13	4	4	3	2UP	3	3	
14	3	3	6	2UP	3	4	
15	4	4	3	2UP	4	3	
16	5	5	5	2UP	5	5	
17	3	3	3	2UP	3	3	
18	4						
IN	36						
TOTAL	72	MATCH RESULT: LANGER/MONTGOMERIE WON (2 & 1)					

SARURDAY – AFTERNOON FOURBALLS

HOLE	PAR	JAMES	RICHARDSON	MATCH POSITION	WADKINS	LEVI	MATCH POSITION
1	4	4	4	1UP	5	5	
2	5	5	4	2UP	5	7	
3	4	4	3	3UP	4	5	
4	4	5	5	2UP	4	4	
5	3	3	3	2UP	3	3	
6	4	4	4	2UP	4	4	
7	5	4		2UP	4	5	
8	3	3		2UP	3	3	
9	4		4	2UP	4		
OUT	36						
10	4	5	4	2UP	4	4	
11	5		4	2UP	4		
12	4	4		2UP	4		
13	4	4	3	3UP	4		
14	3	3		3UP	3		
15	4	4		3UP		4	
16	5	C		2UP	W		
17	3	W	3	3UP	C		
18	4						
IN	36						
TOTAL	72	MATCH RESULT: JAMES/RICHARDSON WON (3 & 1)					

141

SARURDAY – AFTERNOON FOURBALLS

HOLE	PAR	BALLESTEROS	OLAZABAL	MATCH POSITION	STEWART	COUPLES	MATCH POSITION
1	4	4	4	SQ	4	4	SQ
2	5	5	4	1UP	6	5	
3	4	4	4	1UP	4	4	
4	4	4	4	1UP	5	4	
5	3	3	3	1UP	3	3	
6	4	4	4	SQ	3	4	SQ
7	5	4			5	3	1UP
8	3	4	3		3	3	1UP
9	4	4	4		4	4	1UP
OUT	36						
10	4	4	4		4	4	1UP
11	5	5	5		6	4	2UP
12	4		4		4	4	2UP
13	4	3	4		4	4	1UP
14	3	3	3		3		1UP
15	4	3	4	SQ		4	SQ
16	5	5	5	SQ	5	5	SQ
17	3	3	3	SQ		3	SQ
18	4	5	4	SQ	4	4	SQ
IN	36						
TOTAL	72	MATCH RESULT: (HALVED)					

Europe 3½ US ½
Overall Match Position **Europe 8 US 8**

desk report and, in the dark, the BBC Television engineers were winding up their gear for another day. In the team room the atmosphere was now much brighter. It had been a wonderful afternoon and I was quick to praise everyone for what they had done, not least Woosie who had knuckled down to his task with Broadhurst. There was a mood of quiet optimism in the air but I did not have too much time to spend with the side because I had to work out my singles draw.

We needed enough clout at the top to get us away to a good start and enough at the end to cope with a crisis should it arise. I had asked Nick, still down on himself about his performance, where he would like to play. Earlier rather than later was his reply, which suited my plan down to the ground as I had pencilled him in to play No. 1. Now I needed him to do for me what Woosnam had done with Paul in the fourballs. I hoped, too, that Woosie would have regained enough confidence to win a first vital Cup singles. We were a long way from winning but the players had responded brilliantly, turning things around to give us the chance not only to hold on to the Cup but also to win the match. Dave Stockton looked less chirpy as we exchanged the draw and I noticed that Nick at No. 1 had drawn Ray Floyd; Seve would be playing the injured Steve Pate; and David Gilford had come out against the player I considered their weakest link – Wayne Levi.

142

Looking down the list I was convinced we could win and as I drove home in the dark to a pasta or steak dinner at the villas I was definitely enjoying the job a lot more. Two thirds of the work was complete.

· 10 ·

Shock after Shock

The Americans had been battling for almost two years to make their side and our fellows had played since early February for the honour of representing Europe; two days into the match the teams were level 8–8. I felt that I had the best golfers and more strength in depth than the Americans; Dave Stockton felt his team had the edge. They wanted victory badly but so did we. All was set for a 'Showdown on the Shore', as it was being billed in the newspapers.

I was interested to read Ken Burger in the Charleston paper say how much the Americans were learning from the Cup experience and from the attitude we had to it and the way we approached it. The Americans, he claimed, were learning to care about winning and were being given a private lesson in coping with what he described as the reality of pressure – not the kind that balances your chequebook but the kind that grips your heart!

This was America's big day. Vice President Dan Quayle was flying in for the closing ceremony, expecting victory of course. The American television people had even managed to get President George Bush, no less, to open their Telecast with the timely reminder that the Cup belonged in the United States. What would they do, I wondered, if they lost! Where would they and their fans disappear to? I hoped we would find out later in the afternoon.

The crowds may not have found it easy to get round the course, but those who had mountaineered on the sand dunes and risked the rattlesnakes had had wonderful value for money. It was as tight as I had predicted and as tough as the team had known it would be.

As Lesley and I breakfasted early that morning at the buffet provided by the Kiawah Island Inn, I was aware that when we won at Muirfield Village we had led going into the final day's singles. I was also aware that we had won only one series of singles – in 1985 – since the team had become European in 1979. Still, I had a strong team and I liked the draw. I really liked it. Glancing down at the pairings, I talked it through with my wife. Faldo to take Floyd – I was comfortable with that. Feherty was just the sort of golfer to rise to the challenge of toppling the US Open champion, Stewart. Montgomerie had the beating, I felt, of the always erratic Calcavecchia, who might miss the steadying influence of a four-somes or fourball partner. I was sure that in what the Americans were calling the match of the day Jose Maria Olazabal would out-gun Azinger who, in fairness, had shown no ill effects of his mid-summer shoulder surgery. I just could not imagine anyone beating Olazabal on his form at Kiawah. He was dedicated, focused, ready to take on and beat anyone. I was just as certain that Richardson, who was enjoying himself, could beat the wiry Pavin who relies so much on his short game and could be caught out when they turned into the wind at the 14th. I was delighted that David Gilford, whose baptism had been such a difficult one, would have the opportunity to end his first Cup appearance with a deserved victory over Wayne Levi, who had not played well for most of the year and had never really got to grips with the Kiawah course. Seve I considered a banker against the injured Pate and I was just as opti-mistic about our chances in the last four games. Broadhurst need not fear O'Meara after the way he had played with Woosnam. Sam Torrance might find it tough against Fred Couples, who was hav-ing as good a Ryder Cup this year for America as he had had a bad one two years earlier, but superfit James had the beating of Lanny Wadkins. If everything went well, Bernhard Langer would proba-bly not be needed in his anchor spot against Irwin. He was there, however, just in case, because of his strong character and his ability to cope with pressure better than most. Of course it was a rose-tinted look at the draw but not that unrealistic. Whereas in the past we had always been in a situation where you knew you could write off some points, the draw had come out well enough for the singles to be as evenly balanced as they could be, and probably tipped in our favour.

I enjoyed my breakfast and headed off to the course to join Steve Rider for an early-morning interview for BBC Television. It was when I was there that the news came through that Steve Pate, who had been hitting the ball a country mile the day before, had been declared unfit and would not be competing in the singles. I could not believe it. It was 8.30 in the morning and suddenly Pate was out of the American line-up. That meant that David Gilford, the player whose name I had put in a sealed envelope the day before to pair up with any American who could not play, would miss the singles. I was devastated for him. He and Pate would go down on the scoresheet as having halved their game, while Seve, whom Pate had originally been scheduled to meet, would now play the man in the draw opposite Gilford's name – Wayne Levi.

146

The withdrawal of Pate had happened very quickly. When I had arrived at the course I noticed there were only 11 games marked on the programme. But Pate's game was there. They had left the Mark James/Lanny Wadkins game off and, while having coffee in the clubhouse with Sir Iain McLaurin who had come with us on Concorde, I pointed this out to Kerry Haigh, the tournament director. I wanted to know if there was any significance in this: were all the Americans fit? He had reported to me at 8.15 that it had been a printer's error and that all the US side were fit and that everyone was playing. Fifteen minutes later Pate, who had been hitting balls with Stockton on the practice range, was out and, to this day, Dave has not spoken to me about it. I was never officially informed. I just heard it second-hand when I was with the BBC and Steve Rider was told the news in his ear-piece.

I had been very happy with the draw at 8.30; at 8.35 I was faced with the prospect of having to tell David that he was sitting it out when I knew he was desperate to win, and prove, a point. I had had to put someone's name in the envelope and it had to be one of the rookies. Montgomerie had just won his fourball match with Langer on Saturday afternoon, Paul Broadhurst had played just once and won once, and Steven Richardson had been playing well, so it could not be him. Feherty was a first-timer but very experienced, which left me with David who had at least played twice, even if he had lost twice, with first Montgomerie and then Faldo. He had had two defeats and I was not sure of his confidence. I felt that he would have won his singles but I could not take the chance on him feeling bad once he got out there. I felt desperately sorry for David because it had happened only once before in Cup history – Mark James had been unable to play in the 1979 singles series and been paired off with Dr Gil Morgan.

The first thing I wanted to do was to see David who had left the villas and was down in the locker room, putting on his shoes and preparing to begin his practice. I met him there, broke the news and he was inconsolable. He sat with his head in his hands. I explained how sorry I was to have to do this to him and how disappointed I was that he was not playing, but I reminded him that he had a great many more Ryder Cup appearances to come and that before he was finished he would have won many points. I told him that my decision had been largely influenced by the fact that he had played twice and Paul Broadhurst only once. He had no alternative but to accept the situation. What could he do? He had been a victim of a system that requires careful consideration before the next Ryder Cup.

147

I left him with his own thoughts and headed for the 1st tee to see all the players off. The crowds were again huge and anyone who has any doubts as to the importance in world golf of the Ryder Cup should have been at Kiawah to savour the atmosphere and appreciate just what a great event it is – head-to-head on a tough course. I loved matchplay and so too do Ballesteros and Olazabal. I had had the impression that Nick, while happy to go off early, had not banked on being put in the top match, but we needed him to get one of the 5½ points the team needed to draw and retain the Cup or the 6 we wanted to win the match. He had a key role to play and he did not let me down on another day when conditions were exceptionally difficult.

Faldo could not have made a better start. He won the first three holes, the 1st with a par, the 2nd with a birdie and the 3rd with a bogey after Floyd, who had captained the team two years earlier and failed to deliver the trophy to the White House, had driven into the tall grass. Faldo's singles record since 1977, when he had made his debut and beat Tom Watson at Lytham, was won 4 lost 3; Floyd's won 3 lost 3. This certainly seemed to be Faldo's day as, after conceding an 18-inch birdie putt to Floyd at the 10th, he promptly rolled in a 20-footer himself for a half. Par at the 11th put Nick four up with seven to play and coasting, I thought, to our first point.

I had dashed over to check on him at the 9th, which was close to the 1st tee, after the last of the singles had hit off. That was the one between Langer and Irwin. Then I looked in on the second game, Feherty against Stewart. It was just as well I was in radio contact because suddenly things started to go wrong in the top game. Nick lost the 12th, and then was not on the green in three at the short 14th where the breeze from the left was stiffening all the time. He lost that one too. When former US Masters, US Open and USPGA champion Floyd, at 49 the oldest man in either team, sank a four-footer at the 16th to prevent Nick winning 3 and 2 and then won back the short 17th, I was worried. I watched, with some relief, as Floyd drove off line at the last and, with Nick hitting the perfect drive and a crisp, perfectly shaped second shot to the heart of the green, I could relax. It was all over and he had done what I had asked him to do. He had not let me or the team down despite the fact he would admit later that he had never felt so much pressure.

His was not the first point we picked up that frantic afternoon before the crowds began chanting 'USA, USA', like spectators at a football match. David Feherty had won three of the first four holes and had gone on to beat Stewart 2 and 1 before Faldo had finished. It had been a good week for Feherty who can now look forward to a lengthy Cup career. He had relished the chance to represent his country and although playing the course, he said, was like being put through a blender three days running, he had emerged with nothing other than his own stature in European golf enhanced. We now led 10½–8½.

While all this was going on my reports on Colin Montgomerie's progress against Mark Calcavecchia had not been encouraging. I could not quite believe that Colin was five down after nine. Although he won back a hole, at four down with four to play I had mentally written off that point, even if Colin had not. Calcavecchia, superb for 14 holes, suddenly collapsed. He triple-bogeyed the 15th and bogeyed the 16th. At the 17th, where I had now stationed myself, he hit a tee shot that would have made any weekend hacker blush and again triple-bogeyed. He had lost all three holes to Montgomerie whose winning par at the last was enough to give us a half. Colin had won the last four holes and we still led by two points 11–9.

My hope that Steve Richardson might earn a point against the hugely demonstrative Pavin, whose behaviour on the final day bordered on the bizarre as he whipped up gallery support by exaggerating every reaction to almost laughing point, was still alive as I began myself to feel the pressure for every member of the team. It is fun coping with pressure but more difficult in a team situation than on your own. Richardson and Pavin were having a rare old scrap. Pavin, small, angular with a moustache; Richardson with a boyish Sandy Lyle look. This was a catch-weight bout – all-square with five to play.

The big fellow dropped a shot at the short 14th to lose the hole. Nearly everyone that afternoon slipped up there, but not Pavin. Par was good enough to give Pavin the 16th too. As I stood at my post at the 17th advising my team of the correct club selection -- a ploy I was entitled to do as captain and one which Dave Stockton cottoned on to – I had still not given up hope of another half. Richardson was two down but on the green and Pavin's ball lay in a waste bunker from where he had no sight of the pin. My hopes for Steve were dashed when, I have to say, the American played a wonderful recovery, securing the half he needed to earn the point to make the score Europe 11, USA 10.

Seve, not without a tiny wobble in the middle of the round, was four up after 11 holes and ran out a 3 and 2 winner over the luckless Levi, but the tension was building all the time. I was happy in the circumstances that I had Tony Jacklin and Manuel Pinero with me. Tony had experienced this four times. He knew how best to handle the pressure a captain feels on the final day as the battle continues to gain the 14½ points that guarantees victory. What I had

149

done for him in previous matches, he was now doing for me. You know, I never saw my captaincy as a one-man job. I had plenty of people helping me – including our PGA officials Bill Done, David Huish, Philip Weaver and Brian Anderson who were only too ready to give me their view on how this team member or that was playing. I had a lot of help. Dave Stockton said he found the captaincy a very lonely job when the match began but I did not find that. You can make the job as lonely as you want it to be but I liked having people around even if, at the end of the day, I had to take the decisions myself.

Still, out on the course our battle continued for those vital points . . . the points we needed to keep the Cup. Paul Broadhurst was beating Mark O'Meara, but down at the bottom of the draw Sam Torrance had slipped to three down after seven in his match against Fred Couples, while Mark James was three down after eight holes to Lanny Wadkins and Bernhard Langer was not getting much change out of Irwin. The problem was we needed 14 points. We had only 12 in the bag. The key matches as I could see them were Woosnam v Beck and Olazabal v Azinger which, as expected, was turning out to be a real battle of wills. If Ollie won, then it would be the boost we needed, the inspiration that might bring further points from Broadhurst, up in his game against O'Meara, Woosnam and Langer at the bottom of the draw. If he lost, it would be a massive encouragement for those Americans still battling away on the course.

Olazabal had been the most accomplished player on view all week. I kept in touch with things on the radio but went out to give him some moral support. There was nothing I could do to help him except advise him it was a 3-iron at the 17th. But I wanted to be there. The players who had finished – Nick, David, Monty, Seve – all went out too to encourage Olazabal in a match of few halved holes. Only the 5th and 8th holes, the two par 3s, were halved going out as they matched each other shot for shot. It was a compelling duel.

The crowds were becoming more and more noisy and then suddenly everyone was looking up at the sky and there was Concorde coming in – it always is a marvellous sight and represents such European one-upmanship. For a moment what was happening on the course became secondary as everyone watched the plane circle and head off to nearby Charleston Airport. It gave me a boost, and I am sure it gave the team and Spaniard Olazabal a lift as well, but I realized at that moment, too, that we had been at Kiawah long enough. We would be ready to go home the next day. We had not come too late. We had timed everything perfectly, and I wanted to get things finished off and get back home.

Azinger had been one up four times in the match and Olazabal once by the time they came to the 12th, where Azinger three putted to let the Spaniard square matters. Could this be the turning point, I wondered? Within a few minutes I got the answer: No! At the 13th, after Ollie had rolled up a 45-foot putt to within inches of the cup, Azinger, cool as you like, sank his 10-footer for a birdie win. If he knew he had holed that putt from the minute he hit it, the slim 31-year-old based in Florida was just as sure he had missed his four-footer for a half at the next. They were square again with four to go, and then three, and the crowd with this game were going wild. Behind them, Torrance and James were continuing to struggle a bit against solid golf from two of the American team's strongest matchplayers. Woosnam was not exactly dominating his game with Beck, Langer was in a bit of trouble against Irwin, but Broadhurst was still winning. Points from Paul and from Olazabal would guarantee the draw.

151

The pressure was claustrophobic. It was a fresh, bright windy day but it seemed as if we were all caught up in a gigantic torture chamber. The Azinger/Olazabal match had a huge gallery with my friend from Barcelona well in evidence with his big flag. As I watched Ollie make a cast-iron par at the 16th, I wondered if, for only the second time, he might go one up, but Azinger holed a downhill eight-footer for a half. He was not going to be beaten.

Olazabal had the honour at the 17th, which can be a problem. If you hit a good one on to the green that is fine, but if you hit a bad shot you give your opponent the chance to play safe and maybe even win the hole with a 4. Jose Maria used a 1-iron and tried to cut it into the flat part of the green off the bunker but it never moved and flew over the bunker and into a nasty lie in the waste area where the spectators had been tramping around. They were far too close too often all week but there was sometimes nowhere else they could go. Back on the tee, Azinger, pumped up, his hair blowing in the breeze coming almost directly into his face, made the green. His margin for error had been mighty slim but his two putts from 50 feet, after Ollie was unable to go for the pin with his recovery, would, for the sixth time, put the American one up. Olazabal needed to win the last to get a half point but he lost the hole. He had been beaten two up. Seve, standing with me, looked on in total disbelief. He could not believe that Ollie had lost but he had – and to some gutsy golf on the day. Maybe if they met half-a-dozen times, said one European supporter in the crowd, Paul would win once. Unfortunately for us this was the time. Olazabal's unbeaten record for the week had gone and so had one of the chances we had to make one of those two points we needed. Back out on the course the Americans were whipping up the crowds but, throughout, our players never got upset. Later, when I saw a re-run on video, I did not like what the American players did that final day.

Back on the 16th, Woosie, just one down to Beck after having lost two of the first three holes and having stuck manfully to the job despite his errant putter, was driving into the water off the tee and en route to maintaining the unenviable record of never having won a Ryder Cup singles in five attempts. Down on the beach Mark Calcavecchia, fearful that his failure to finish off Colin Montgomerie might cost America the Cup, was trying, as he put it, to regroup. His wife Sheryl, who sometimes caddies for him, reminded him that the Ryder Cup was a team game and that there were 10 other fellows chasing points as well . . . the same points we were after!

When Woosie lost to Beck, who had been rested from the second day because of his first-day form, the scores were tied at 12-12, but we went ahead again when Broadhurst rolled in with a 3 and 1 victory over O'Meara. He had played twice and won twice, never letting O'Meara recover from making bogeys and losing three of the first five holes. O'Meara hit his tee shot at the 17th into the water and elected to walk to the right round the lake. He had no idea Paul's ball, off the green, had ended in such a horrid lie that it would have been easy for him to skim it into the water. When O'Meara put his third in the pond and waved his arms in surrender, I told Paul to go and shake his hand as quickly as possible.

Frankly I was amazed no American had checked Paul's lie.

The rookies had done well and Broadhurst should become a permanent fixture in Cup teams. But which of the three experienced men left on the course was going to squeeze out the other point we needed? Not Sam Torrance, who went down 3 and 2 to Fred Couples who, making full amends for having lost a crucial point to Christy O'Connor Jnr during the 1989 draw at The Belfry, would emerge as the Americans' most successful points scorer, and not Mark James. Despite battling through to the 16th after being four down at the turn, he lost to the irrepressible Wadkins about whom I had had doubts! Lanny could still be in there pitching for the US in two years' time.

The Wadkins/James game did not end without an incident that epitomized just how the tension was affecting some of us as the match drew to its desperately close finish. James, two down, hit his third through the green at the 16th and into an unplayable lie in a crevice in the sand. When I got there the official observer with the game – an American – informed me that a spectator had kicked James's ball into the bad spot. 'Was the ball lying well before he kicked it?' I asked, but he hardly got a chance to answer. Payne Stewart, who, having lost, was now operating as an American cheerleader and who had dashed over to see how James's ball was lying, butted in. He took exception to my question and accused me of putting words into the observer's mouth. Of course I was not doing anything of the sort and pointed out firmly that I was trying to ascertain the facts. James did get to replace the ball and later, when the match was over, Payne came to the team trailer to apologize for his behaviour, admitting he was out of line. I knew it was just the charged-up atmosphere that had got to him. I have always been a firm admirer of Payne and his readiness to admit he was wrong only puts me in higher regard of the US Open champion.

153

So, with the score reading Europe 13, USA 14, only Bernhard Langer could produce the vital point that would enable us to keep the Cup. At the 14th hole of his match with Hale Irwin he had missed a short putt to go two down but into the left-to-right wind and with Irwin tiring we all went out to cheer him in. The crowds, who had been pleasantly boisterous the day before, were now sensing victory. The thought that within half-an-hour America would have the Cup back was causing them to chant almost continuously, making concentration difficult for both players as the tension became almost unbearable. Hale Irwin would later say that he could hardly breathe.

Langer, in the anchor position, I knew was feeling it and I was wondering to myself if I could ever go through with it again! I went back to catch up with the man who was our only hope to avoid defeat. He remained totally professional, deliberate, thorough. Nothing was rushed. Nothing needed to be rushed. If he could win three of the last four holes – a tall order for anyone other than Bernhard – we would still have the Cup in our luggage when we headed home on Concorde. Spirits rose as Langer's par was good enough to win him back the 15th. They both parred the 16th in the tough weather conditions and frightening tension. Then we had more to cheer when Langer won back the 17th where 46-year-old Irwin, clearly feeling the pressure, missed a short putt – the kind he had holed with nonchalant ease earlier in the match.

Seve wanted to help Langer so much that he suggested that I go on to the green at the 17th to tell him the line of the putt, which I was entitled to do, but I did nothing. I told Seve that it would just add to the pressure on Bernhard who actually did hole without his or my help. Can you imagine my going forward in front of 20,000 people to tell him the line? In fact my mind went back to Florida in 1983 again when Jack Nicklaus had looked so incongruous going on the greens to help one of his team with the line. Both had got it wrong. Jack came out of that poorly. I believed that the captain should let the player and the caddie get on with it – but Seve was so charged up. We were all charged up. It was so close.

Now they were all-square and Bernhard had ensured that the destination of the Cup would not be decided until the very last putt. The dedicated German was, after all, fulfilling the very role that I had cast him for but hoped he would never have to play. Incredible, I thought, that two teams should be so evenly matched that probably a draw was fair. Yet as we all walked up the hill to the 18th tee, giving the committed Langer and the anxious Irwin space to settle themselves for two crucial drives and the big finale, I knew what a draw would mean. Could Langer, now on the tee, concentrating as television cameramen and press photographers jockeyed for the best positions – could he complete his fightback? Could he dig even deeper into his reserves and manage somehow to win one more hole?

As I had walked with him to the 18th tee he had said nothing. He was concentrating totally. His drive down the last was perfect. Irwin hooked wildly into the crowd but so deep were the spectators that the ball bounced clear and on to the fairway. Both were short and right of the green in two, with Irwin to play first. Tiring, he mishit his pitch and came up 12 feet short. Some of the team members around me could not look as Bernhard asked for relief from not one but two sprinkler heads. He would have been able to get relief in Europe but the PGA of America official would have none of it; in America there is no relief in this situation. He putted and his ball bounced off one of them, skipped up and on some six feet past the hole. He had holed crucial putts of slightly longer length on the run in, including that one at the 17th. Now he would face the ultimate putt to decide the Ryder Cup if Irwin did not hole his 12-footer. Irwin missed. His ball finished 12 inches away and Langer generously conceded the putt.

Now the spotlight turned on Langer. He began, with caddie Peter Coleman, to discuss the line. A spike mark or two added to the complications. At first, they were not in complete agreement. Langer thought it left lip and Coleman just inside the left lip. Around the green we could hardly breathe. The team had battled for three long hard days on as tough a course as the Ryder Cup has ever been played and it had all come down to one putt on the last green of the last game. If Bernhard holed it was a draw and we kept the Cup. If he missed America had won by a point. My own mind went back to the day at Palm Beach Gardens in 1983 when I was in the same position – on the 17th green in the last game against Tom Watson. My decision to have Bernhard as anchor had paid off. His courage had seen him through to this point and now he needed to have luck on his side one more time. His wife Vicki was there watching as he stood over the ball. The line, the weight had to be just right. The spike mark, unable under the rules to be tapped down, just added to his problems. Now he and Coleman were agreed. It was a left-lip putt but it might be deflected by one of the spike marks. It was safer they felt to aim just inside the left edge of the Cup.

155

Suddenly, as if someone had switched off the sound, there was silence, not total silence because over to the right the Atlantic Ocean was still crashing in on the beach. The galleries were hushed. It was the moment when Stockton's carefully planned campaign could end in defeat. Thousands of spectators around the green, straining to see the putt, and millions more in 23 countries, saw Langer adjust his grip – that grip which has him clutching his putter shaft and left forearm with his right hand. He steadied himself. No one dared breathe as he took the club back smoothly without a jerk and struck the ball on the exact line he and Coleman had chosen. It hit the right edge and finished a few inches away. The moment it missed, the place went wild and Langer was frozen like a statue, his face contorted in anguish.

The Americans had won and their celebrations began instantly. Television cameramen moved in and around us trying to get inter-views with them, not with us. The American wives were leaping around. For a moment it was dangerous; I thought someone might get injured. A relieved Irwin hugged Langer who, broken-hearted, moved quickly off the green towards the team trailer with the rest of the side consoling him. There were tears in his eyes as I grabbed him. Words were unnecessary. I then pushed my way through to captain Stockton. There were tears in his eyes as well, but his were of joy. He had welded his team into a cohesive unit, just as Tony Jacklin had the Europeans in the previous four matches and hope-fully I had at Kiawah. It was a magnificent team win as far as he was concerned, planned over months and executed in three drama-charged days. Mark Calcavecchia was back off the beach and looking happier now. Payne Stewart whispered to him that his half point against Montgomerie had been vital. He smiled the smile of a man who will still have something to prove in two years' time.

Lesley and I headed back through the crowds to the caravan. Inside, Langer, the stoic of the links, was crying, as were Seve, Tony Jacklin and Nick – not just because we had lost but because we all felt so badly for Bernhard who had had to face up to that six-footer that had meant so much to so many. Mark James was trying to put things into perspective and wee Woosie was endeavouring in his own way to cheer everyone up. He jumped up on the table and shouted out, 'Right, that's it. Now we are going to beat them in two

SUNDAY – SINGLES

HOLE	PAR	FALDO	MATCH POSITION	FLOYD	MATCH POSITION
1	4	4	1UP	5	
2	5	4	2UP	5	
3	4	5	3UP	6	
4	4	4	3UP	4	
5	3	4	2UP	3	
6	4	5	1UP	4	
7	5	3	2UP	5	
8	3	2	3UP	3	
9	4	4	3UP	4	
OUT	36				
10	4	3	3UP	3	
11	5	4	4UP	5	
12	4	5	3UP	4	
13	4	4	3UP	4	
14	3	C	2UP	W	
15	4	5	2UP	5	
16	5	4	2UP	4	
17	3	4	1UP	3	
18	4	4	2UP	5	
IN	36				
TOTAL	72	MATCH RESULT: FALDO WON (2-UP)			

HOLE	PAR	FEHERTY	MATCH POSITION	STEWART	MATCH POSITION
1	4	4	1UP	5	
2	5	4	2UP	6	
3	4	4	2UP	4	
4	4	4	3UP	5	
5	3	3	3UP	3	
6	4	5	2UP	3	
7	5	4	2UP	4	
8	3	3	2UP	3	
9	4	4	2UP	4	
OUT	36				
10	4	4	2UP	4	
11	5	5	3UP	6	
12	4	4	3UP	4	
13	4	4	4UP	5	
14	3	3	4UP	3	
15	4	5	3UP	4	
16	5	6	2UP	5	
17	3	3	2UP	3	
18	4				
IN	36				
TOTAL	72	MATCH RESULT: FEHERTY WON (2 & 1)			

HOLE	PAR	MONTGOMERIE	MATCH POSITION	CALCAVECCHIA	MATCH POSITION
1	4	4		3	1UP
2	5	6		5	2UP
3	4	4		6	1UP
4	4	6		4	2UP
5	3	4		4	2UP
6	4	4		4	2UP
7	5	5		4	3UP
8	3	4		3	4UP
9	4	5		3	5UP
OUT	36				
10	4	3		4	4UP
11	5	4		5	3UP
12	4	4		4	3UP
13	4	4		4	3UP
14	3	C		W	4UP
15	4	5		7	3UP
16	5	5		6	2UP
17	3	5		6	1UP
18	4	4	SQ	5	SQ
IN	36				
TOTAL	72	MATCH RESULT: (HALVED)			

157

SUNDAY – SINGLES

HOLE	PAR	OLAZABAL	MATCH POSITION	AZINGER	MATCH POSITION
1	4	4		3	1UP
2	5	W	SQ	C	SQ
3	4	3	1UP	4	
4	4	6	SQ	5	SQ
5	3	3	SQ	3	SQ
6	4	4		3	1UP
7	5	5	SQ	6	SQ
8	3	3	SQ	3	SQ
9	4	5		4	1UP
OUT	36				
10	4	3	SQ	4	SQ
11	5	C		W	1UP
12	4	4	SQ	5	SQ
13	4	4		3	1UP
14	3	3	SQ	4	SQ
15	4	5	SQ	5	SQ
16	5	5	SQ	5	SQ
17	3	4		3	1UP
18	4	C		W	2UP
IN	36				
TOTAL	72	MATCH RESULT: AZINGER WON (2-UP)			

SUNDAY – SINGLES

HOLE	PAR	RICHARDSON	MATCH POSITION	PAVIN	MATCH POSITION
1	4	3	1UP	4	
2	5	5	SQ	4	SQ
3	4	C		W	1UP
4	4	5		4	2UP
5	3	4		4	2UP
6	4	4		5	1UP
7	5	5		4	2UP
8	3	3		3	2UP
9	4	5		5	2UP
OUT	36				
10	4	4		4	2UP
11	5	5		6	1UP
12	4	4		4	1UP
13	4	4	SQ	5	SQ
14	3	4		3	1UP
15	4	4		4	1UP
16	5	6		5	2UP
17	3	3		3	2UP
18	4				
IN	36				
TOTAL	72	MATCH RESULT: PAVIN WON (2 &1)			

SUNDAY – SINGLES

HOLE	PAR	BALLESTEROS	MATCH POSITION	LEVI	MATCH POSITION
1	4	4	SQ	4	SQ
2	5	7	1UP	8	
3	4	3	2UP	4	
4	4	4	2UP	4	
5	3	3	2UP	3	
6	4	4	2UP	4	
7	5	5	1UP	4	
8	3	2	2UP	4	
9	4	3	3UP	4	
OUT	36				
10	4	4	3UP	4	
11	5	W	4UP	C	
12	4	4	4UP	4	
13	4	4	3UP	3	
14	3	3	3UP	3	
15	4	5	2UP	4	
16	5	5	3UP	6	
17	3				
18	4				
IN	36				
TOTAL	72	MATCH RESULT: BALLESTEROS WON (3 & 2)			

158

SUNDAY – SINGLES

HOLE	PAR	WOOSNAM	MATCH POSITION	BECK	MATCH POSITION
1	4	4	SQ	4	SQ
2	5	5		4	1UP
3	4	5		4	2UP
4	4	W		C	1UP
5	3	3	SQ	4	SQ
6	4	4	SQ	4	SQ
7	5	5	SQ	5	SQ
8	3	3		2	1UP
9	4	4	SQ	5	SQ
OUT	36				
10	4	4	SQ	4	SQ
11	5	4		3	1UP
12	4	4		4	1UP
13	4	4		4	1UP
14	3	4		4	1UP
15	4	5		5	1UP
16	5	C		W	2UP
17	3	C		W	3UP
18	4				
IN	36				
TOTAL	72	MATCH RESULT: BECK WON (3 & 1)			

SUNDAY – SINGLES

HOLE	PAR	BROADHURST	MATCH POSITION	O'MEARA	MATCH POSITION
1	4	4	SQ	4	SQ
2	5	6		5	1UP
3	4	4	SQ	5	SQ
4	4	4	1UP	5	
5	3	3	2UP	4	
6	4	4	2UP	4	
7	5	5	2UP	5	
8	3	2	3UP	3	
9	4	4	3UP	4	
OUT	36				
10	4	5	2UP	4	
11	5	5	3UP	6	
12	4	4	3UP	4	
13	4	4	2UP	3	
14	3	3	2UP	3	
15	4	4	2UP	4	
16	5	5	2UP	5	
17	3	2	3UP	C	
18	4				
IN	36				
TOTAL	72	MATCH RESULT: BROADHURST WON (3 & 1)			

159

SUNDAY – SINGLES

HOLE	PAR	TORRANCE	MATCH POSITION	COUPLES	MATCH POSITION
1	4	5		4	1UP
2	5	5		5	1UP
3	4	4		4	1UP
4	4	4		4	1UP
5	3	4		4	1UP
6	4	5		4	2UP
7	5	5		4	3UP
8	3	3		3	3UP
9	4	4		4	3UP
OUT	36				
10	4	4		4	3UP
11	5	6		5	4UP
12	4	5		4	5UP
13	4	4		5	4UP
14	3	4		5	3UP
15	4	5		5	3UP
16	5	5		5	3UP
17	3				
18	4				
IN	36				
TOTAL	72	MATCH RESULT: COUPLES WON (3 & 2)			

SUNDAY – SINGLES

HOLE	PAR	JAMES	MATCH POSITION	WADKINS	MATCH POSITION
1	4	4	1UP	5	
2	5	C	SQ	4	SQ
3	4	5		4	1UP
4	4	5		5	1UP
5	3	3		2	2UP
6	4	4		4	2UP
7	5	5		5	2UP
8	3	4		3	3UP
9	4	6		5	4UP
OUT	36				
10	4	4		5	3UP
11	5	5		5	3UP
12	4	4		4	3UP
13	4	4		5	2UP
14	3	3		2	3UP
15	4	4		5	2UP
16	5	6		5	3UP
17	3				
18	4				
IN	36				
TOTAL	72	MATCH RESULT: WADKINS WON (3 & 2)			

HOLE	PAR	LANGER	MATCH POSITION	IRWIN	MATCH POSITION
1	4	5		4	1UP
2	5	C		W	2UP
3	4	W		C	1UP
4	4	4		4	1UP
5	3	4		4	1UP
6	4	3	SQ	4	SQ
7	5	5	SQ	5	SQ
8	3	4		3	1UP
9	4	4		3	2UP
OUT	36				
10	4	4		4	2UP
11	5	5		6	1UP
12	4	4		4	1UP
13	4	4		4	1UP
14	3	5		4	2UP
15	4	4		5	1UP
16	5	5		5	1UP
17	3	3	SQ	4	SQ
18	4	5	SQ	5	SQ
IN	36				
TOTAL	72	MATCH RESULT: (HALVED)			

Europe 5½ US 6½
Final Result **Europe 13½ US 14½**

years' time', helping to change the atmosphere because everyone cheered – especially Jose Maria who looked as if he would never be able to wait two years to get his revenge. His look was the blackest of all. Over in one corner a few caddies, drained by the week's efforts and saddened, too, by our ever so narrow defeat, were also tearful and some of the wives were wiping away tears too. It was hard for me not to be tearful as well. I wanted to be but felt, as captain, I should not let myself cry.

There were inevitably interviews afterwards and then the presentation ceremony in which the PGA of America had arranged for the Vice President to present the Cup to Dave Stockton. This annoyed me, as had the Gulf War scenario during the week, and, even if it was undiplomatic, I told Dan Quayle when he joined us for the presentation that I wanted to remind him that we in Britain and in Europe had had servicemen killed in the Gulf War too. I must say he looked a bit bemused but I could see he was a nice chap who chatted in the team trailer with us before we left for the closing ceremony. We had all recovered our composure. The match had been closely fought and we had lost. The victory meant a lot to America and maybe a great deal more for the future of the Cup itself. It also meant that we would be hungrier than ever to get it back in two years' time, when we are back at a venue where we have never lost – The Belfry.

Tony Jacklin said to me quietly that in some respects the result might not turn out too badly for us. He was concerned that if we had won again it might have jeopardized the future of the Cup once more; that the Americans might even stop playing us because they do not like getting beaten all the time! I did not exactly share his point of view but I could see what he was aiming at as we headed back to the practice range for the final chapter in the Ryder Cup that had, for me, been as exciting and as novel as my first one as a player in 1969. Up on the presentation dais and before the flags were lowered, I said my piece. I congratulated the Americans and promised them a hard-fought battle next time, and then I picked up the Cup which I had carried in four days earlier and walked across to present it to Dave. As my team applauded I shook the hand of every one of the Americans before returning to my place on the platform. Stockton put the Cup back on the podium and, not to be outdone, Dan Quayle then re-presented it to Dave a few minutes later – but I had made my point.

After the presentation ceremony I had things to do. I attended the final press conference but I had asked the team to meet me in my apartment later so that we could go together to the final dinner – the victory dinner. Meanwhile, some of the players slipped away to join the British fans in the hospitality tents and Sam and Ian even managed to persuade Bernhard Langer to go along. When he went into the tent he was given a tremendous cheer. There were a great many American fans there as well and they were loving it

161

too. It was a very happy occasion and there was a tremendous spirit of friendliness. Of course at this time the American players, euphoric in victory, were tossing their captain Dave Stockton into the Atlantic! I somehow doubt that my team would have done that to me.

Recent dinners have been sombre occasions because the Americans have not won. They take defeat so badly. Our team, in contrast, knew how to lose although I would not want them to get too accustomed to it. I said a few words, telling Dave to keep the Cup well polished because we aimed to take it back in two years' time, and Lesley and I had a reasonably early night after having a final drink with some of the team in my apartment.

We might not have arrived at Kiawah as a team but we were going back as one and we had to be out of Kiawah early in the morning in order to get Concorde back to Heathrow. We were sorry we had not won but we had enjoyed the week tremendously. So saying, we were all glad, in a way, that the week was over, although most of the fellows were going straight on to Bernhard Langer's own tournament – the Mercedes German Masters – in which, ironically, one of his invited guest players was going to be Hale Irwin.

When we arrived in London on that Monday night, the Wentworth Club had sent a delegation with banners to welcome the team home. That was nice. Sky, BBC and ITV were all there to welcome us back and there was one last interview to do. It had been a hard, tough week and I knew it would take me a few days to unwind and let the realization of what had happened sink in, but I was proud of the team, even in defeat – maybe especially in defeat.

162

11

Forward with Pride

When the match ended at Kiawah, one of the first questions I was asked was whether or not I would accept the captaincy again if it was offered to me. The players had certainly made it clear that I had done the job to their satisfaction by giving me a total vote of confidence, but at the end-of-match press conference I was fairly circumspect, saying that the matter was something I would have to think over very carefully.

I wanted to have a week to recover. I did not want to be drawn into making a decision either way in the heat of the moment, neither would I have wished to have tempted fate by making that decision public. There were the views of the PGA to consider, and I certainly wanted to consult the Wentworth Club board before making any announcement. I know how pleased they were when I was first appointed captain, feeling that it could only benefit the club, but would they be so supportive second time round? And even if everybody was firmly behind my reappointment, did I in fact want to expose myself and my family to another two years in the limelight? I needed to think it through.

I never said it at the time, but from the moment I was given the honour of captaining the Ryder Cup side I had felt under pressure. In public I took the line that it was easy taking over from Tony, but deep down I knew how difficult it was going to be to follow someone who had done such a marvellous job. Quite apart from the attendant problems of captaining the side in a foreign – I hesitate to say hostile – environment, I was obviously worried about making the wrong decisions and had not really known how Seve and the others would take to my being the captain. At Kiawah I felt I was under as much pressure as the new Cup men. I was a rookie captain concerned not only with the team's performance but also my own. Yet it could have been more difficult.

I think what helped me take over from Tony was the fact that I knew the players all so well. I was around when Seve joined the Tour in 1974, I have won tournaments with Nick and Ian in the field, I was there when Bernhard emerged on the scene. I like to think that I was a friend as well as a captain.

I had been determined we should all be open about everything. I wanted nothing bottled up and had told the team that I did not want to hear any criticism about this or that long after something could have been done about it. I talked to them privately and told them that if they were worried about their games, their partners in fourball or foursomes, the food, the arrangements at the villas, their caddies – anything – they should come to me immediately. My door, I told them, would always be open, but fortunately there were no crises. The team knew mine was a consensus captaincy. I had always felt that the most successful captains – and I include here Eric Brown – were those who involved the team, taking the players along with them. My own style reflected that feeling.

When it came to the crunch, everyone on the team helped me relax and in so doing enabled me to do the job as well as I could. So saying, during the final afternoon's play, perhaps because the pressure was at its worst, I told myself that I did not want to do it again. The captaincy takes up a huge slice of your life and you have to handle a lot of responsibility for many months prior to Cup week. I felt that the team and I had performed well, but I wondered then, as the crowds milled around and we battled for that final half point that would let us keep the Cup, whether, maybe, I had had my crack at it and that that should be that. I had made some mistakes and

164

got a lot right, but should I now be thinking of turning away from the Cup and concentrating much more on my role at Wentworth?

After a few days, when I was back home and looking at things more objectively away from the drama of that last day, I realized that if the Tour and PGA officials and players wanted me to carry on I almost had a duty to do so, although I do not see the Ryder Cup captaincy as a career for me in the way it became for Tony Jacklin, who was just not allowed to give it up. I wondered whether the PGA officials might see things differently, however, from the team members and the Tour. I certainly did not want a repeat performance of what had happened two years earlier, but then I remembered that we now operate the Cup in partnership and that the behind-the-scenes fighting is over.

I had noticed how well the partnership went at Kiawah, something I was determined to strengthen wherever I could. The PGA officials had taken exception in the past to the fact that Tony had kept the team room absolutely private. He had not allowed any of them in, but I told them that they were as welcome in the trailer as the Tour officials. I made no distinction between them. They had come a long way to support the team and had every right, I felt, to have access to us in the trailer. Anyway, much of our private chatting was done in the villas.

165

The officials all knew what their roles were at Kaiwah, and for the first time in ages all got on superbly well, which had certainly not been the case at The Belfry. This unity was endorsed by Ken Schofield on our journey home. Speaking to us from Concorde's cockpit, he thanked the patrons for supporting the side and the players for their tremendous efforts. He said that irrespective of the result it had been a happy Ryder Cup, a great week for European golf in which, importantly, 'all the PGA and Tour officials have worked as well off the course supporting the team as the players have done well on it'. Although John Lindsey did not speak, Ken had indicated to him the substance of what he was going to say and the PGA executive director was in full agreement with the sentiments.

My decision to accept the captaincy, if offered, was strengthened when a letter arrived from John Lindsey, expressing the wish, I felt, that I should carry on. It reflected the new united approach to the

Cup relationship. I was rather flattered, too, by the post-match comments in the PGA trade journal which I receive as a club professional. Philip Weaver, the chairman, talked in his monthly letter about how well the team had played and behaved: 'The graciousness in defeat shown by captain Gallacher and his courageous team and the magnanimity of his closing ceremony remarks clearly illustrate that whilst he remains captain the ethics and dignity of the European Ryder Cup side are in safe hands. We'll lick our wounds and look forward to The Belfry in 1993 when together with the Tour and our hugely stylish sponsors Johnnie Walker we will welcome the American team to contest the 30th series of Ryder Cup matches.'

It made me think again of the dispute we had had. You know, most of the Tour board comprises club professionals, who are also members of the PGA. None of us ever wanted the PGA to go out of business. Yet they had not been able to believe or understand that at the time.

After my return, the letters flooded in – dozens and dozens of them. Peter Alliss sent me a lovely note and that really did please me. We had been on opposite sides during the dispute. He had felt he needed to be the voice of the PGA standing up to the Tour, whom he saw as the big bad bully. Of course it was not that way at all. He said how much he had enjoyed the match and how impressed he had been at the way the team had stood up to the pressure and had behaved so properly. Getting that letter meant a great deal to me, as did those from our showbusiness friends Russ Abbot, Jimmy Tarbuck and Bruce Forsyth, who lives nearby. Others came from Sir Neil Macfarlane, the former Minister of Sport, the Earl of Stockton and Sir Iain McLaurin, who is a strong supporter of golf and who had been with us at Kiawah. Then there was the letter from singer-composer Chris de Burgh who had been at The Belfry in 1989 and who sent me a marvellous poem. There were letters from some of the Tour players and from several of the American team, which was rather nice, plus letters from fans all over the world who had watched the match on television or been at Kiawah. I should like to thank all of them for taking the trouble to write to congratulate the team and for wishing them all the very best next time.

166

Everyone is happy to be at The Belfry in 1993 and the new more friendly atmosphere is such a bonus as far as the captain is concerned. The performance of the team at Kiawah makes me confident about the chances of success in 1993. I was never in doubt that we could beat the Americans, even with five rookies in the side, because I knew how good the younger players were. We came within a point of winning with five newcomers and there will be plenty more of similar calibre vying for places in two years' time, thanks to the tremendous competition on the constantly expanding European Tour. David Gilford will get his chance again in the future, and I cannot imagine that we could ever play a Cup match again with Nick Faldo and Ian Woosnam collecting only two points between them . . . and I imply no criticism nor do I apportion any blame by saying that. We will need their valuable experience in two years' time.

I really do believe that Dave Stockton and his team had a good week at Kiawah. His men putted slightly better on those Bermuda greens, which they are more used to than us, but we were not outplayed. Only an inch or two prevented us from retaining the Cup. We can of course do much better. Our foursomes play, despite more practice than usual, was abysmally poor and we need to find a way of reversing that trend. These days, however, we go to America on equal terms and that should give all of us in Europe a tremendous sense of pride. We know we can win in America and, more importantly, so do the Americans. Muirfield Village was not a one-off surprise achieved because that year we were on some sort of 'high'. We shall win again in America because we are good now and getting better all the time.

Now comes the inquest, with the possibility of changes to the rules. One of the greatest difficulties I found at Kiawah was having to leave four people out in each of the four series over the first two days. I did not like it from the team's point of view and I believe it is unfair on the public who come to see the best golfers in action, and then find one third of them sitting it out. I will therefore be putting forward a proposal that there should in future be five foursomes and fourballs each day instead of four, on the basis that two rested players per series is perfectly adequate. In the past, keeping down the number of available points was important because we did

167

not, as a team, have strength in depth. Tony Jacklin believed very strongly that no changes should be made to the format, but today I believe there is no need to protect our 'tail' at the expense of the paying public.

We need also to look seriously at ways of guaranteeing there will always be 12 games on the final day, even if that means taking a reserve with us for use on that day only. I still feel for David Gilford who, having built himself up for a key single, had his hopes dashed just an hour before he was scheduled to tee off.

Finally, I do feel that our points-collecting events should include those at the end of the previous season, when some of our biggest tournaments are played. The European Open, the European Masters, the German Masters, the Lancôme Trophy and, of course, the Volvo Masters – tournaments which attract the strongest fields – have had no bearing in the past on the final points table. That seems to me to be wrong. The players with the best chance of making the side should be those who do best in our most prestigious events which, with additional Ryder Cup importance, would become even more important than they already are.

168

As for me, I have learned so much about so many things that the experience has benefited me considerably. I know we did not win but the important thing to remember is our confidence has not been dented by events at Kiawah. We did not like losing, but losing the way we did – so narrowly and with such dignity – was not so bad. America regained their self respect but only just. They are sure to be worried at the prospect of taking us on at The Belfry.

Just after the Cup had been won and lost, when we were all so emotional in the team caravan, I told the players to remember how hurt they were at that moment. Outside, the Americans were rejoicing and gloating in their hour of triumph. I asked them to remember in two years' time what it felt like getting beaten and why, when they got the chance to put matters right at The Belfry, they should not lack the will and determination to complete the job. The Ryder Cup, I reminded them, did not belong in the USA. They knew that anyway.

Looking round the caravan I saw 12 tired and wounded players, each desperate, I knew, to be a member of the 1993 European side charged with the task of winning back the Cup. I think I knew then that, given the opportunity, I would be proud to lead them again despite my natural caution to commit myself at that time.

Dave Stockton wanted to keep his job but lost out. Tom Watson is the man the PGA of America has chosen to lead their team in 1993. His captaincy will be different in character to that of Stockton. Tom has nothing to prove and he seems determined to remind his players about the tradition that surrounds the Ryder Cup. That is something I wholeheartedly support.

Kiawah was just another reminder to us all of the importance of the match, the enviable position it enjoys in world golf and how rewarding it is in a spiritual sense to all who are fortunate to have taken part. How grateful we all are that Samuel Ryder stayed for tea that afternoon at Wentworth 65 years ago.

169

The Course

Kiawah Island, 10 miles long and 1½ miles at its widest point, is where Pete Dye built the Ocean course for the 29th Ryder Cup. For him, it was Project No. 63. 'After this,' he said, 'I may go back to my original job – insurance. There is nothing more for me to do in golf-course building. I will never get another chance like this one at Kiawah.' What attracted Dye to the project was that 10 holes – 5 through 9 and 14 through 18 – run east to west along the ocean.

The course depends much for its difficulty on the wind and, because it can blow strongly from several directions, Dye built his course with multiple tees. From the front tees the course can be as short as 5294 yards; from the back it is 7756 yards. Yet it was never meant to be played to its full length. It is set up each day using tees that take the wind direction into consideration, to afford players the most comfortable test. Comfortable in Ocean terms is still mighty difficult.

If the wind is coming from the west, the holes from 5 through 13 are testing. The rest are downwind. If the wind is in the east, the opening four and the closing five are the toughest, as was the case during the Ryder Cup. The variety and number of the tees available for play can be judged by looking at the short 17th. You can play that green from a series of teeing grounds extended through 90 degrees – depending on the wind direction and the tee used. You could find yourself using a driver or a 7-iron.

Dye produced a remarkable course which tested a player's ability to hit accurate long-iron seconds in the wind and his skill at playing delicate approach shots to sloping greens, often set at an angle to the fairway. It also tested patience and, in the end, was a worthy setting for one of the most dramatic Ryder Cups in the match's 64 years' history.

KEY TO MAPS

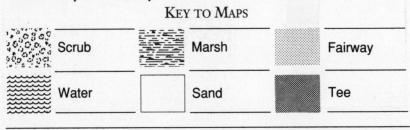

Scrub	Marsh	Fairway
Water	Sand	Tee

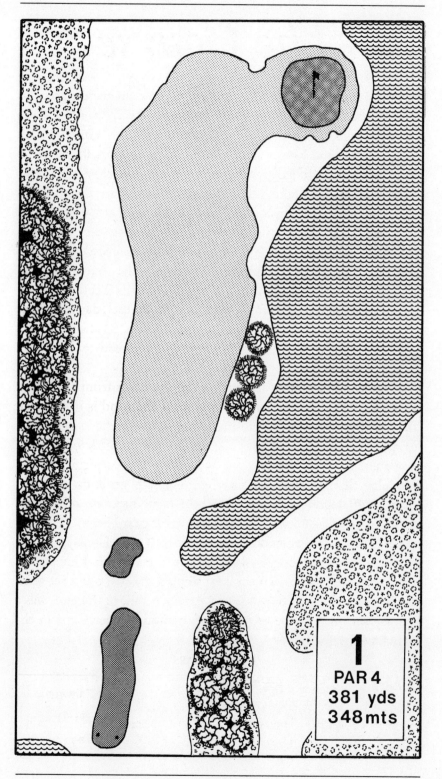

1
PAR 4
381 yds
348 mts

172

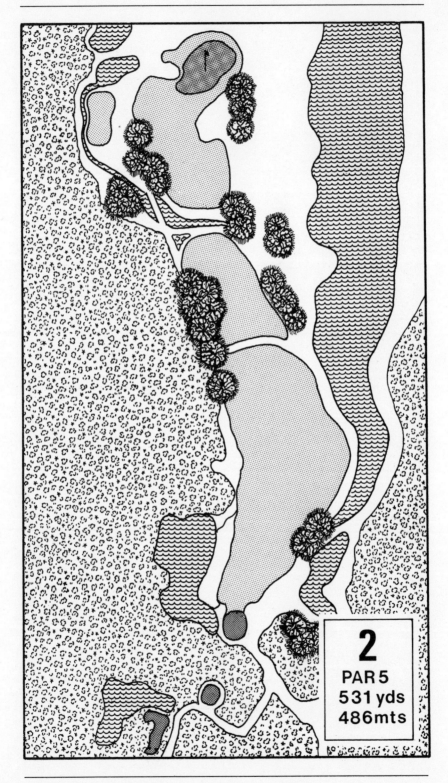

2
PAR 5
531 yds
486mts

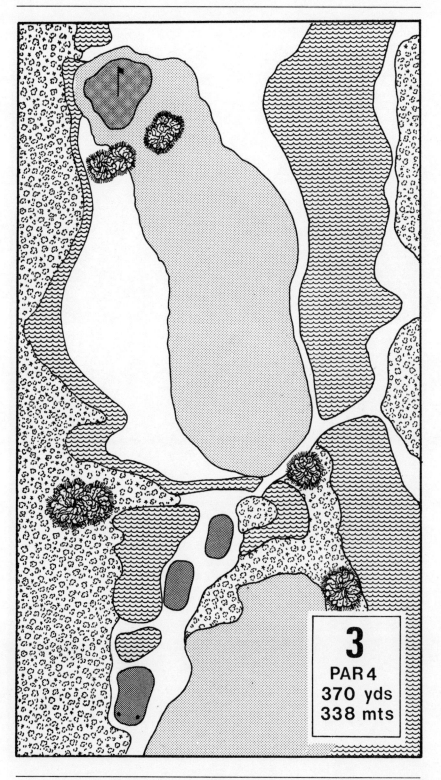

173

3
PAR 4
370 yds
338 mts

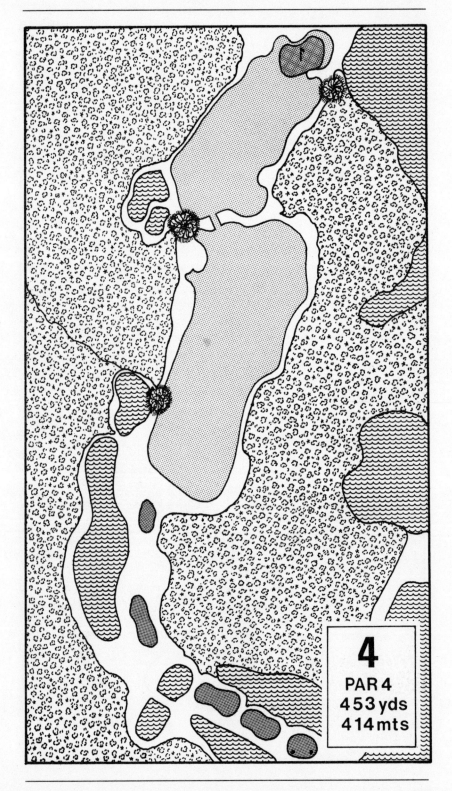

174

4

PAR 4
453 yds
414 mts

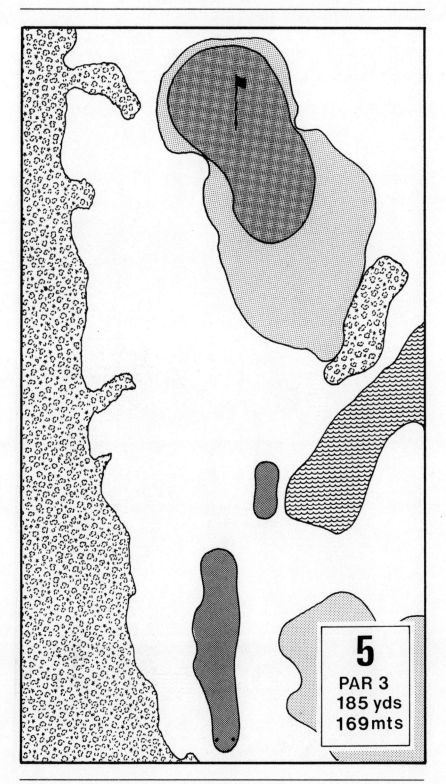

175

5
PAR 3
185 yds
169mts

176

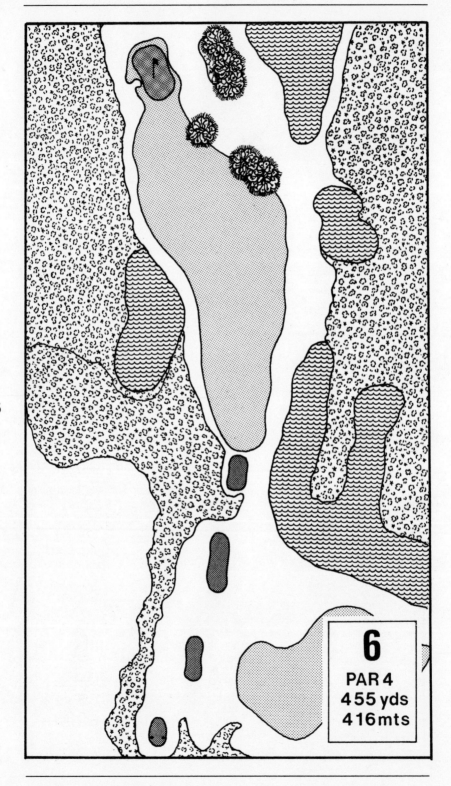

6
PAR 4
455 yds
416 mts

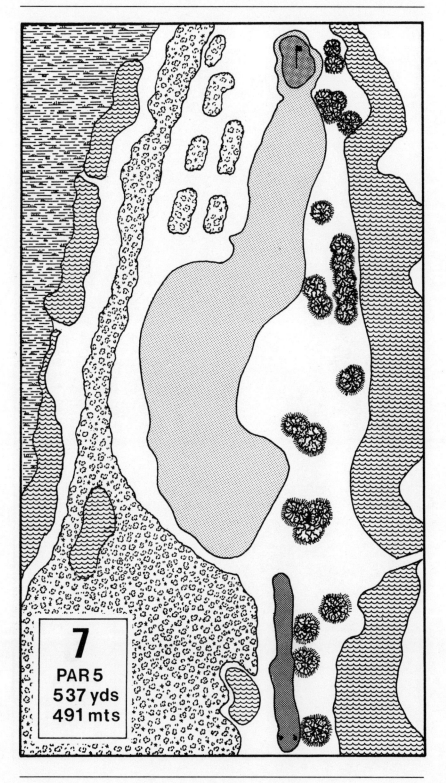

7
PAR 5
537 yds
491 mts

178

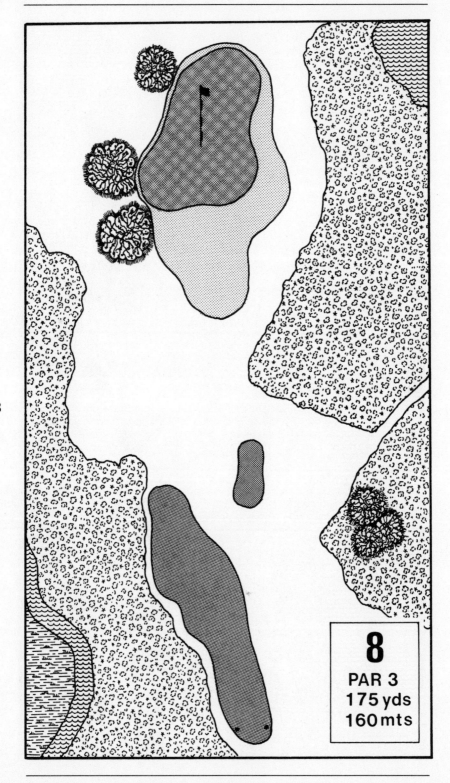

8
PAR 3
175 yds
160 mts

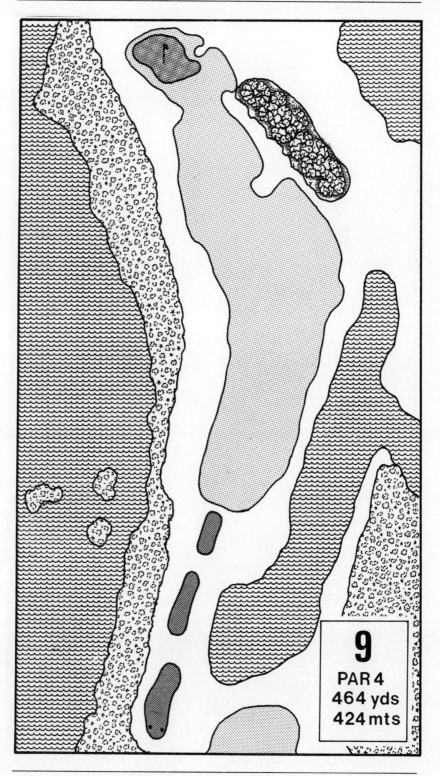

179

9

PAR 4
464 yds
424 mts

180

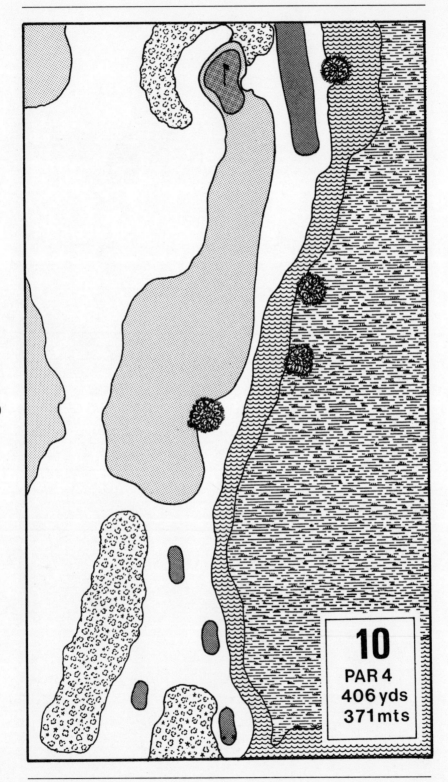

10
PAR 4
406 yds
371 mts

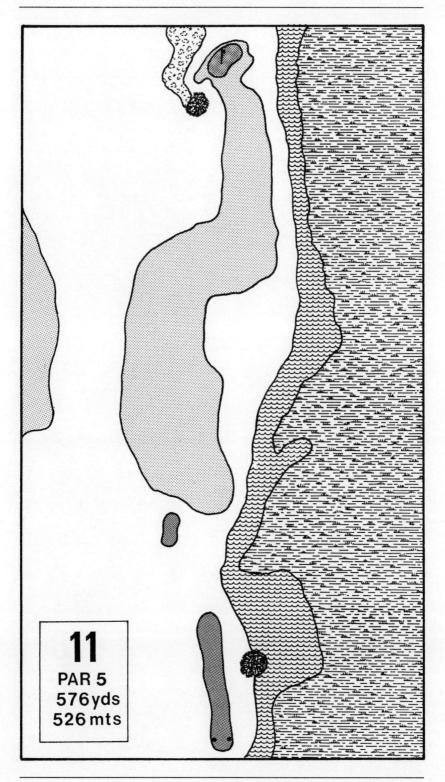

11
PAR 5
576 yds
526 mts

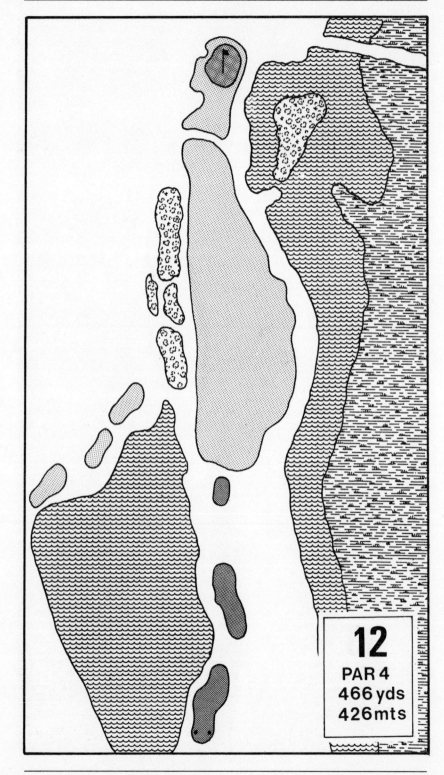

182

12
PAR 4
466 yds
426 mts

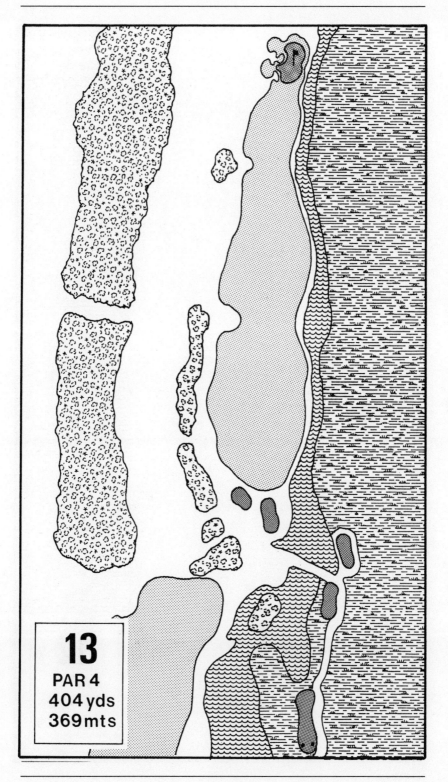

13
PAR 4
404 yds
369 mts

184

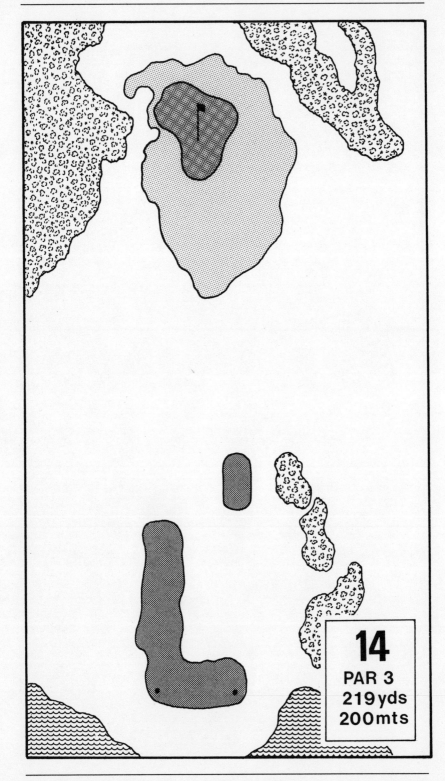

14
PAR 3
219 yds
200 mts

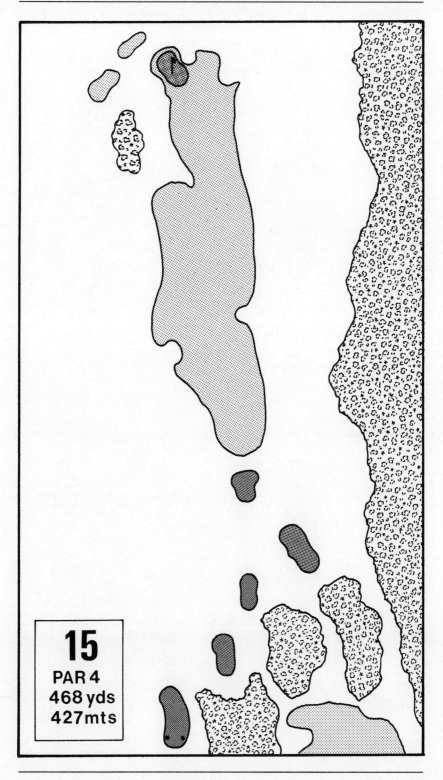

185

15
PAR 4
468 yds
427mts

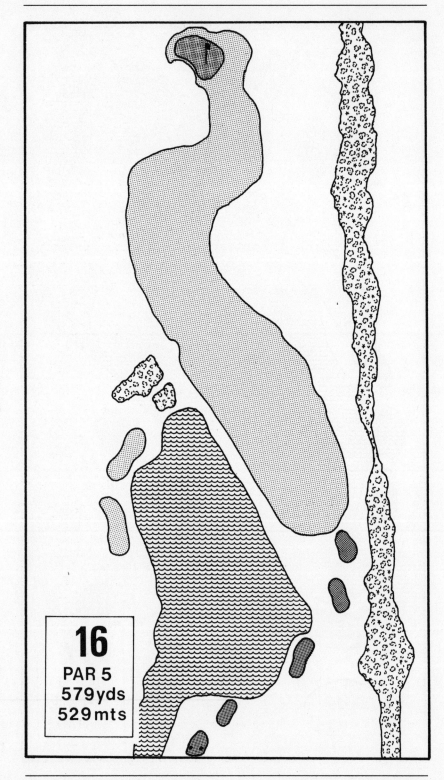

16
PAR 5
579yds
529mts

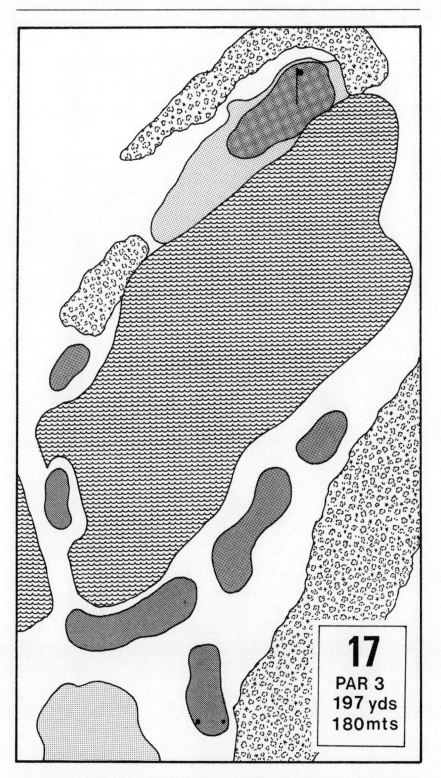

187

17
PAR 3
197 yds
180mts

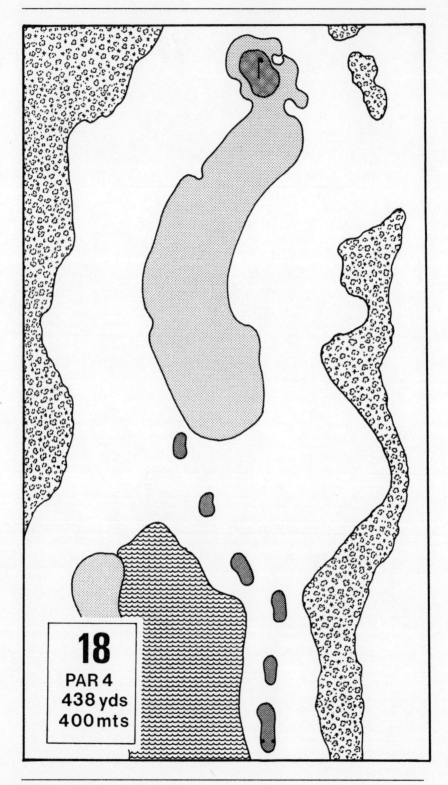

Scorecards

FRIDAY - MORNING FOURSOMES

HOLE	PAR	BALLESTEROS/ OLAZABAL	MATCH POSITION	AZINGER/ BECK	MATCH POSITION
1	4	4	SQ	4	SQ
2	5	8		4	1UP
3	4	4		4	1UP
4	4	6		6	1UP
5	3	4		3	2UP
6	4	4		4	2UP
7	5	5		5	2UP
8	3	3		3	2UP
9	4	5		4	3UP
OUT	36				
10	4	4		5	2UP
11	5	5		5	2UP
12	4	3		4	1UP
13	4	3	SQ	4	SQ
14	3	3	SQ	3	SQ
15	4	4	1UP	5	
16	5	5	1UP	5	
17	3	2	2UP	3	
18	4				
IN	36				
TOTAL	72	MATCH RESULT: BALLESTEROS/OLAZABAL WON (2 & 1)			

HOLE	PAR	LANGER/ JAMES	MATCH POSITION	FLOYD/ COUPLES	MATCH POSITION
1	4	5		4	1UP
2	5	5	SQ	6	SQ
3	4	4	SQ	4	SQ
4	4	5	SQ	5	SQ
5	3	3		2	1UP
6	4	6		4	2UP
7	5	5		5	2UP
8	3	3		2	3UP
9	4	4		4	3UP
OUT	36				
10	4	5		4	4UP
11	5	4		4	4UP
12	4	4		5	3UP
13	4	3		5	2UP
14	3	3		5	1UP
15	4	4		4	1UP
16	5	6		5	2UP
17	3	3		3	2UP
18	4				
IN	36				
TOTAL	72	MATCH RESULT: FLOYD/COUPLES WON (2 & 1)			

FRIDAY - MORNING FOURSOMES

HOLE	PAR	GILFORD/ MONTGOMERIE	MATCH POSITION	WADKINS/ IRWIN	MATCH POSITION
1	4	5		3	1UP
2	5	4		4	1UP
3	4	C		W	2UP
4	4	5		5	2UP
5	3	3		2	3UP
6	4	5		4	4UP
7	5	W		C	3UP
8	3	3		2	4UP
9	4	4		4	4UP
OUT	36				
10	4	4		4	4UP
11	5	6		5	5UP
12	4	4		4	5UP
13	4	5		5	5UP
14	3	4		5	4UP
15	4	5		6	3UP
16	5	C		W	4UP
17	3				
18	4				
IN	36				
TOTAL	72	MATCH RESULT: WADKINS/IRWIN WON (4 & 2)			

FRIDAY - MORNING FOURSOMES

HOLE	PAR	FALDO/ WOOSNAM	MATCH POSITION	STEWART/ CALCAVECCHIA	MATCH POSITION
1	4	4	SQ	4	SQ
2	5	5		4	1UP
3	4	4		4	1UP
4	4	C		W	2UP
5	3	4		4	2UP
6	4	4		5	1UP
7	5	5		5	1UP
8	3	3		3	1UP
9	4	4		4	1UP
OUT	36				
10	4	4		4	1UP
11	5	4	SQ	5	SQ
12	4	5		4	1UP
13	4	4		3	2UP
14	3	3		3	2UP
15	4	4		4	2UP
16	5	5		5	2UP
17	3	W		C	1UP
18	4	4		4	1UP
IN	36				
TOTAL	72	MATCH RESULT: STEWART/CALCAVECCHIA WON (1-UP)			

FRIDAY - AFTERNOON FOURBALLS

HOLE	PAR	TORRANCE	FEHERTY	MATCH POSITION	WADKINS	O'MEARA	MATCH POSITION
1	4	4	4	SQ		4	SQ
2	5		6		4		1UP
3	4	4	4		4	4	1UP
4	4	4	4		4	4	1UP
5	3	3	4		3	3	1UP
6	4	4	4		4	4	1UP
7	5	4	4		5	4	1UP
8	3	4	4		3	3	2UP
9	4	4	5		3	3	3UP
OUT	36						
10	4	4	4		4	4	3UP
11	5	4	4		5	5	2UP
12	4	4	5		4	4	2UP
13	4	4	5		4	4	2UP
14	3	4	2		3	3	1UP
15	4	4	4		4	4	1UP
16	5	5	5		5	5	1UP
17	3	2	3		3	2	1UP
18	4	5	4	SQ	5	5	SQ
IN	36						
TOTAL	72	MATCH RESULT: (HALVED)					

FRIDAY - AFTERNOON FOURBALLS

HOLE	PAR	BALLESTEROS	OLAZABAL	MATCH POSITION	AZINGER	BECK	MATCH POSITION
1	4	4	5	SQ	4	4	SQ
2	5	6	5	SQ		5	SQ
3	4	4	4		3	4	1UP
4	4	4	4		4	4	1UP
5	3	3	2	SQ	3	3	SQ
6	4	4	4		3	4	1UP
7	5	4	5	SQ	5	5	SQ
8	3	2	3	1UP	3	3	
9	4	5	4	1UP	4	5	
OUT	36						
10	4	4	3	1UP	3	4	
11	5	5	4	1UP	4	5	
12	4	5	4	1UP		4	
13	4		4	SQ	3	4	SQ
14	3	2	3	1UP	3	3	
15	4	4	4	1UP	4	4	
16	5	5	4	1UP	4	4	
17	3	3		2UP	5		
18	4						
IN	36						
TOTAL	72	MATCH RESULT: BALLESTEROS/OLAZABAL WON (2 & 1)					

FRIDAY - AFTERNOON FOURBALLS

HOLE	PAR	RICHARDSON	JAMES	MATCH POSITION	PAVIN	CALCAVECCHIA	MATCH POSITION
1	4	4	4	SQ	4	4	SQ
2	5		4	1UP	5		
3	4	5	3	2UP	4	5	
4	4	4	4	2UP	4	4	
5	3		3	2UP	3	3	
6	4	3		3UP	4	4	
7	5	3		4UP		4	
8	3	3	3	3UP	2		
9	4	5	5	2UP	4	4	
OUT	36						
10	4	4	4	2UP	4	4	
11	5	4	5	3UP	5	5	
12	4	4		4UP	5		
13	4	4	4	4UP	4	4	
14	3	4	3	5UP	4	4	
15	4						
16	5						
17	3						
18	4						
IN	36						
TOTAL	72	MATCH RESULT: RICHARDSON/JAMES WON (5 & 4)					

FRIDAY - AFTERNOON FOURBALLS

HOLE	PAR	FALDO	WOOSNAM	MATCH POSITION	FLOYD	COUPLES	MATCH POSITION
1	4	4	4		5	3	1UP
2	5	6	6		5	5	2UP
3	4	4	3		4	4	1UP
4	4	4	3	SQ	4	4	SQ
5	3	3	3	SQ	3	4	SQ
6	4	4	4		3	4	1UP
7	5	4	5		5	4	1UP
8	3	2	3	SQ	3	3	SQ
9	4	4	4	SQ	4	4	SQ
OUT	36						
10	4	4	4		3	4	1UP
11	5	5	5		4	5	2UP
12	4	4	4		4	3	3UP
13	4	4	4		5	3	4UP
14	3	3	3		3	4	4UP
15	4	4	4		4	3	5UP
16	5						
17	3						
18	4						
IN	36						
TOTAL	72	MATCH RESULT: FLOYD/COUPLES WON (5 & 3)					

SATURDAY - MORNING FOURSOMES

HOLE	PAR	FEHERTY/ TORRANCE	MATCH POSITION	WADKINS/ IRWIN	MATCH POSITION
1	4	4	1UP	6	
2	5	6	SQ	5	SQ
3	4	4	1UP	5	
4	4	4	1UP	4	
5	3	3	1UP	3	
6	4	5	SQ	4	SQ
7	5	4	SQ	4	SQ
8	3	4		3	1UP
9	4	4	SQ	5	SQ
OUT	36				
10	4	4		3	1UP
11	5	6		6	1UP
12	4	5		4	2UP
13	4	4		5	1UP
14	3	5		4	2UP
15	4	5		4	3UP
16	5	C		W	4UP
17	3				
18	4				
IN	36				
TOTAL	72	MATCH RESULT: WADKINS/IRWIN WON (4 & 2)			

SATURDAY - MORNING FOURSOMES

HOLE	PAR	JAMES/ RICHARDSON	MATCH POSITION	CALCAVECCHIA/ STEWART	MATCH POSITION
1	4	4	1UP	5	
2	5	6	SQ	5	SQ
3	4	5		4	1UP
4	4	4		4	1UP
5	3	3	SQ	4	SQ
6	4	4	SQ	4	SQ
7	5	4	1UP	5	
8	3	3	SQ	2	SQ
9	4	4		3	1UP
OUT	36				
10	4	5		4	2UP
11	5	5		6	1UP
12	4	5		3	2UP
13	4	4		4	2UP
14	3	3		3	2UP
15	4	4		4	2UP
16	5	6		6	2UP
17	3	W		C	1UP
18	4	5		5	1UP
IN	36				
TOTAL	72	MATCH RESULT: CALCAVECCHIA/STEWART WON (1-UP)			

SATURDAY - MORNING FOURSOMES

HOLE	PAR	FALDO/ GILFORD	MATCH POSITION	AZINGER/ O'MEARA	MATCH POSITION
1	4	5		3	1UP
2	5	5		5	1UP
3	4	5		4	2UP
4	4	5		5	2UP
5	3	3		2	3UP
6	4	5		4	4UP
7	5	C		W	5UP
8	3	3		3	5UP
9	4	5		5	5UP
OUT	36				
10	4	4		3	6UP
11	5	5		5	6UP
12	4	C		W	7UP
13	4				
14	3				
15	4				
16	5				
17	3				
18	4				
IN	36				
TOTAL	72	MATCH RESULT: AZINGER/O'MEARA WON (7 & 6)			

SATURDAY - MORNING FOURSOMES

HOLE	PAR	BALLESTEROS/OLAZABAL	MATCH POSITION	FLOYD/COUPLES	MATCH POSITION
1	4	5		4	1UP
2	5	5		5	1UP
3	4	4	SQ	5	SQ
4	4	4	SQ	4	SQ
5	3	2	1UP	3	
6	4	4	2UP	5	
7	5	4	2UP	4	
8	3	3	2UP	3	
9	4	4	3UP	5	
OUT	36				
10	4	4	3UP	4	
11	5	5	3UP	5	
12	4	4	3UP	4	
13	4	4	3UP	4	
14	3	3	4UP	4	
15	4	5	3UP	4	
16	5	6	3UP	6	
17	3				
18	4				
IN	36				
TOTAL	72	MATCH RESULT: BALLESTEROS/OLAZABAL WON (3 & 2)			

SATURDAY - AFTERNOON FOURBALLS

HOLE	PAR	WOOSNAM	BROADHURST	MATCH POSITION	AZINGER	IRWIN	MATCH POSITION
1	4	4	4	SQ	5	4	SQ
2	5	6	6		5	5	1UP
3	4		4		4	4	1UP
4	4	4	4		4	4	1UP
5	3	3			3		1UP
6	4	4			4		1UP
7	5		4		5	4	1UP
8	3	3	3	SQ	4	4	SQ
9	4	5	C		3	4	1UP
OUT	36						
10	4	W	3	SQ	C	C	SQ
11	5	5	6	SQ	5		SQ
12	4	4	4	SQ	4	4	SQ
13	4	4	3	1UP	4	4	
14	3	4	3	1UP	3	4	
15	4	5	5	1UP	6	5	
16	5	5		1UP	5	5	
17	3	3		2UP	4	C	
18	4						
IN	36						
TOTAL	72	MATCH RESULT: WOOSNAM/BROADHURST WON (2 & 1)					

SATURDAY - AFTERNOON FOURBALLS

HOLE	PAR	LANGER	MONTGOMERIE	MATCH POSITION	PAVIN	PATE	MATCH POSITION
1	4	4	4	SQ	4	6	SQ
2	5	5	5	SQ	5	5	SQ
3	4	4	4	SQ	5	4	SQ
4	4	3	4	1UP	4	5	
5	3	3	3	1UP	3	3	
6	4	4	5	1UP	5	4	
7	5	4	4	2UP	6	5	
8	3	4	4	1UP	4	3	
9	4	5	5	SQ	5	4	SQ
OUT	36						
10	4	4	5	1UP	5	5	
11	5	5	5	1UP	5	6	
12	4	4	4	2UP	5	5	
13	4	4	3	2UP	3	3	
14	3	3	6	2UP	3	4	
15	4	4	3	2UP	4	3	
16	5	5	5	2UP	5	5	
17	3	3	3	2UP	3	3	
18	4						
IN	36						
TOTAL	72	MATCH RESULT: LANGER/MONTGOMERIE WON (2 & 1)					

SATURDAY - AFTERNOON FOURBALLS

HOLE	PAR	JAMES	RICHARDSON	MATCH POSITION	WADKINS	LEVI	MATCH POSITION
1	4	4	4	1UP	5	5	
2	5	5	4	2UP	5	7	
3	4	4	3	3UP	4	5	
4	4	5	5	2UP	4	4	
5	3	3	3	2UP	3	3	
6	4	4	4	2UP	4	4	
7	5	4		2UP	4	5	
8	3	3		2UP	3	3	
9	4		4	2UP	4		
OUT	36						
10	4	5	4	2UP	4	4	
11	5		4	2UP	4		
12	4	4		2UP	4		
13	4	4	3	3UP	4		
14	3	3		3UP	3		
15	4	4		3UP		4	
16	5	C		2UP	W		
17	3	W	3	3UP	C		
18	4						
IN	36						
TOTAL	72	MATCH RESULT: JAMES/RICHARDSON WON (3 & 1)					

SATURDAY - AFTERNOON FOURBALLS

HOLE	PAR	BALLESTEROS	OLAZABAL	MATCH POSITION	STEWART	COUPLES	MATCH POSITION
1	4	4	4	SQ	4	4	SQ
2	5	5	4	1UP	6	5	
3	4	4	4	1UP	4	4	
4	4	4	4	1UP	5	4	
5	3	3	3	1UP	3	3	
6	4	4	4	SQ	3	4	SQ
7	5	4			5	3	1UP
8	3	4	3		3	3	1UP
9	4	4	4		4	4	1UP
OUT	36						
10	4	4	4		4	4	1UP
11	5	5	5		6	4	2UP
12	4		4		4	4	2UP
13	4	3	4		4	4	1UP
14	3	3	3		3		1UP
15	4	3	4	SQ		4	SQ
16	5	5	5	SQ	5	5	SQ
17	3	3	3	SQ		3	SQ
18	4	5	4	SQ	4	4	SQ
IN	36						
TOTAL	72	MATCH RESULT: (HALVED)					

SUNDAY - SINGLES

HOLE	PAR	FALDO	MATCH POSITION	FLOYD	MATCH POSITION
1	4	4	1UP	5	
2	5	4	2UP	5	
3	4	5	3UP	6	
4	4	4	3UP	4	
5	3	4	2UP	3	
6	4	5	1UP	4	
7	5	3	2UP	5	
8	3	2	3UP	3	
9	4	4	3UP	4	
OUT	36				
10	4	3	3UP	3	
11	5	4	4UP	5	
12	4	5	3UP	4	
13	4	4	3UP	4	
14	3	C	2UP	W	
15	4	5	2UP	5	
16	5	4	2UP	4	
17	3	4	1UP	3	
18	4	4	2UP	5	
IN	36				
TOTAL	72	MATCH RESULT: FALDO WON (2-UP)			

194

195

SUNDAY - SINGLES

HOLE	PAR	FEHERTY	MATCH POSITION	STEWART	MATCH POSITION
1	4	4	1UP	5	
2	5	4	2UP	6	
3	4	4	2UP	4	
4	4	4	3UP	5	
5	3	3	3UP	3	
6	4	5	2UP	3	
7	5	4	2UP	4	
8	3	3	2UP	3	
9	4	4	2UP	4	
OUT	36				
10	4	4	2UP	4	
11	5	5	3UP	6	
12	4	4	3UP	4	
13	4	4	4UP	5	
14	3	3	4UP	3	
15	4	5	3UP	4	
16	5	6	2UP	5	
17	3	3	2UP	3	
18	4				
IN	36				
TOTAL	72	MATCH RESULT: FEHERTY WON (2 & 1)			

SUNDAY - SINGLES

HOLE	PAR	MONTGOMERIE	MATCH POSITION	CALCAVECCHIA	MATCH POSITION
1	4	4		3	1UP
2	5	6		5	2UP
3	4	4		6	1UP
4	4	6		4	2UP
5	3	4		4	2UP
6	4	4		4	2UP
7	5	5		4	3UP
8	3	4		3	4UP
9	4	5		3	5UP
OUT	36				
10	4	3		4	4UP
11	5	4		5	3UP
12	4	4		4	3UP
13	4	4		4	3UP
14	3	C		W	4UP
15	4	5		7	3UP
16	5	5		6	2UP
17	3	5		6	1UP
18	4	4	SQ	5	SQ
IN	36				
TOTAL	72	MATCH RESULT: (HALVED)			

SUNDAY - SINGLES

HOLE	PAR	OLAZABAL	MATCH POSITION	AZINGER	MATCH POSITION
1	4	4		3	1UP
2	5	W	SQ	C	SQ
3	4	3	1UP	4	
4	4	6	SQ	5	SQ
5	3	3	SQ	3	SQ
6	4	4		3	1UP
7	5	5	SQ	6	SQ
8	3	3	SQ	3	SQ
9	4	5		4	1UP
OUT	36				
10	4	3	SQ	4	SQ
11	5	C		W	1UP
12	4	4	SQ	5	SQ
13	4	4		3	1UP
14	3	3	SQ	4	SQ
15	4	5	SQ	5	SQ
16	5	5	SQ	5	SQ
17	3	4		3	1UP
18	4	C		W	2UP
IN	36				
TOTAL	72	MATCH RESULT: AZINGER WON (2-UP)			

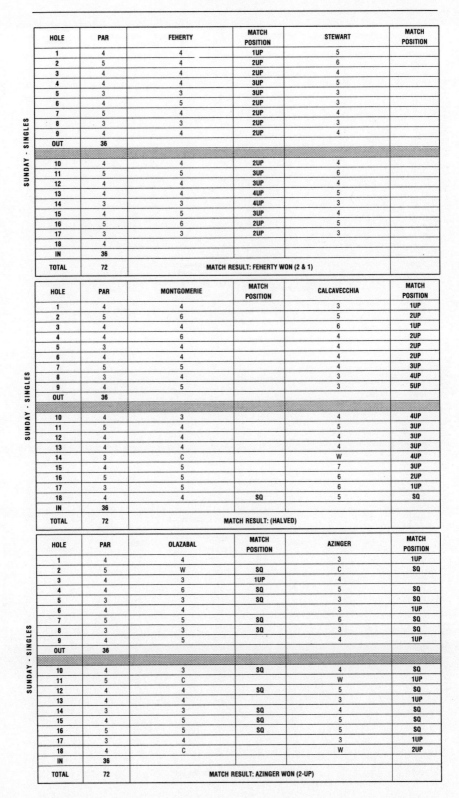

196

SUNDAY - SINGLES

HOLE	PAR	RICHARDSON	MATCH POSITION	PAVIN	MATCH POSITION
1	4	3	1UP	4	
2	5	5	SQ	4	SQ
3	4	C		W	1UP
4	4	5		4	2UP
5	3	4		4	2UP
6	4	4		5	1UP
7	5	5		4	2UP
8	3	3		3	2UP
9	4	5		5	2UP
OUT	36				
10	4	4		4	2UP
11	5	5		6	1UP
12	4	4		4	1UP
13	4	4	SQ	5	SQ
14	3	4		3	1UP
15	4	4		4	1UP
16	5	6		5	2UP
17	3	3		3	2UP
18	4				
IN	36				
TOTAL	72	MATCH RESULT: PAVIN WON (2 &1)			

HOLE	PAR	BALLESTEROS	MATCH POSITION	LEVI	MATCH POSITION
1	4	4	SQ	4	SQ
2	5	7	1UP	8	
3	4	3	2UP	4	
4	4	4	2UP	4	
5	3	3	2UP	3	
6	4	4	2UP	4	
7	5	5	1UP	4	
8	3	2	2UP	4	
9	4	3	3UP	4	
OUT	36				
10	4	4	3UP	4	
11	5	W	4UP	C	
12	4	4	4UP	4	
13	4	4	3UP	3	
14	3	3	3UP	3	
15	4	5	2UP	4	
16	5	5	3UP	6	
17	3				
18	4				
IN	36				
TOTAL	72	MATCH RESULT: BALLESTEROS WON (3 & 2)			

HOLE	PAR	WOOSNAM	MATCH POSITION	BECK	MATCH POSITION
1	4	4	SQ	4	SQ
2	5	5		4	1UP
3	4	5		4	2UP
4	4	W		C	1UP
5	3	3	SQ	4	SQ
6	4	4	SQ	4	SQ
7	5	5	SQ	5	SQ
8	3	3		2	1UP
9	4	4	SQ	5	SQ
OUT	36				
10	4	4	SQ	4	SQ
11	5	4		3	1UP
12	4	4		4	1UP
13	4	4		4	1UP
14	3	4		4	1UP
15	4	5		5	1UP
16	5	C		W	2UP
17	3	C		W	3UP
18	4				
IN	36				
TOTAL	72	MATCH RESULT: BECK WON (3 & 1)			

SUNDAY - SINGLES

HOLE	PAR	BROADHURST	MATCH POSITION	O'MEARA	MATCH POSITION
1	4	4	SQ	4	SQ
2	5	6		5	1UP
3	4	4	SQ	5	SQ
4	4	4	1UP	5	
5	3	3	2UP	4	
6	4	4	2UP	4	
7	5	5	2UP	5	
8	3	2	3UP	3	
9	4	4	3UP	4	
OUT	36				
10	4	5	2UP	4	
11	5	5	3UP	6	
12	4	4	3UP	4	
13	4	4	2UP	3	
14	3	3	2UP	3	
15	4	4	2UP	4	
16	5	5	2UP	5	
17	3	2	3UP	C	
18	4				
IN	36				
TOTAL	72	MATCH RESULT: BROADHURST WON (3 & 1)			

HOLE	PAR	TORRANCE	MATCH POSITION	COUPLES	MATCH POSITION
1	4	5		4	1UP
2	5	5		5	1UP
3	4	4		4	1UP
4	4	4		4	1UP
5	3	4		4	1UP
6	4	5		4	2UP
7	5	5		4	3UP
8	3	3		3	3UP
9	4	4		4	3UP
OUT	36				
10	4	4		4	3UP
11	5	6		5	4UP
12	4	5		4	5UP
13	4	4		5	4UP
14	3	4		5	3UP
15	4	5		5	3UP
16	5	5		5	3UP
17	3				
18	4				
IN	36				
TOTAL	72	MATCH RESULT: COUPLES WON (3 & 2)			

HOLE	PAR	JAMES	MATCH POSITION	WADKINS	MATCH POSITION
1	4	4	1UP	5	
2	5	C	SQ	4	SQ
3	4	5		4	1UP
4	4	5		5	1UP
5	3	3		2	2UP
6	4	4		4	2UP
7	5	5		5	2UP
8	3	4		3	3UP
9	4	6		5	4UP
OUT	36				
10	4	4		5	3UP
11	5	5		5	3UP
12	4	4		4	3UP
13	4	4		5	2UP
14	3	3		2	3UP
15	4	4		5	2UP
16	5	6		5	3UP
17	3				
18	4				
IN	36				
TOTAL	72	MATCH RESULT: WADKINS WON (3 & 2)			

HOLE	PAR	LANGER	MATCH POSITION	IRWIN	MATCH POSITION
1	4	5		4	1UP
2	5	C		W	2UP
3	4	W		C	1UP
4	4	4		4	1UP
5	3	4		4	1UP
6	4	3	SQ	4	SQ
7	5	5	SQ	5	SQ
8	3	4		3	1UP
9	4	4		3	2UP
OUT	36				
10	4	4		4	2UP
11	5	5		6	1UP
12	4	4		4	1UP
13	4	4		4	1UP
14	3	5		4	2UP
15	4	4		5	1UP
16	5	5		5	1UP
17	3	3	SQ	4	SQ
18	4	5	SQ	5	SQ
IN	36				
TOTAL	72	MATCH RESULT: (HALVED)			

SUNDAY - SINGLES

198

Index

199

Jones, Robert Trent, *61*
Keiser, Herman, *14*
King, Sam, *14*
Kite, Tom, *20, 56-7*
Langer, Bernhard, *20, 25,
33, 58, 61-3, 68, 71, 76,
79, 84, 92-3, 95, 105-9,
113, 115, 117, 119, 124,
126, 137-8, 145, 147-8,
150-1, 153-6, 161-2, 164*
Leadbetter, David, *63, 93*
Levi, Wayne, *57-8, 137,
142, 145-6, 149*
Lindsey, John, *31, 33,
48-50, 54, 165*
Lyle, Sandy, *20, 25, 71, 73,
77-8, 149*
Macfarlane, Sir Neil, *166*
McLaurin, Sir Iain, *146,
166*
McLean, Michael, *62-3*
McNulty, Mark, *73-5*
Martin, Miguel Angel, *63,
67*
Miller, Frank, *93*
Mills, Peter, *15*
Mitchell, Abe, *10-1*
Montgomerie, Colin, *64,
68, 71, 75, 92-3, 105,
107-8, 113, 115, 118-9,
126, 132, 137-8, 145,
147-9, 152, 156*
Morgan, Dr Gil, *56-7, 147*
Nicklaus, Jack, *9, 13, 17,
19-22, 26, 37, 40, 55,
57-8, 65, 88, 90, 154*
Norman, Greg, *58*
O'Connor Snr, Christy, *15,
96*
O'Connor Jnr, Christy, *22,
77, 153*
Olazabal, Jose Maria, *22,
43, 51, 58, 61, 66-7, 69,
70, 73, 76-7, 79, 92-3,
105-7, 109, 113, 115-8,
123, 126, 128-9, 131, 133,
137, 139-40, 145, 147,
151-2, 160*
O'Meara, Mark, *57-8, 121,*

*124, 128, 130, 145, 150,
152*
Oosterhuis, Peter, *18-9*
Palmer, Arnold, *9, 16, 18,
114*
Pate, Steve, *57-8, 95-6, 105,
108, 114, 126, 137-8, 142,
145-6*
Pavin, Corey, *57-8, 95,
121-2, 137-8, 145, 149*
Pavin, Shannon, *95-6*
Persson, Magnus, *63*
Pinero, Manuel, *26, 31,
114, 118, 149*
Quayle, Dan, *144, 161*
Rafferty, Ronan, *22, 71, 73,
78*
Ralph, Glenn, *78-9*
Rees, Dai, *12, 15, 17, 26, 96*
Renwick, Dave, *131*
Richardson, Steven, *60-1,
63, 65, 71, 74, 92-3,
105-8, 121-2, 126, 128,
132-3, 137, 139, 145, 147,
149*
Rider, Steve, *33, 146*
Rivero, Jose, *66-7, 79*
Rocca, Costantino, *67-9*
Rogers, Bill, *20*
Romero, Eduardo, *63, 66*
Ross, Ian, *49*
Ryder, Samuel, *10-2, 14-5,
17, 27, 96, 109, 110, 169*
Sarazen, Gene, *13*
Schofield, Ken, *20, 25, 32,
34, 48-9, 54, 69, 118, 165*
Scott, Tom, *15*
Shrewsbury, John, *136*
Simpson, John, *79*
Simpson, Tim, *56-7, 96,
105*
Smith, Dick, *95*
Snead, Sam, *17, 20*
Stewart, Payne, *43, 51, 58,
68, 109, 114, 119, 128,
132-3, 137, 140, 145, 148,
153, 156*
Still, Ken, *17, 86*
Stockton, Dave, *17, 41-7,*

*52, 56-8, 69, 83-4, 87,
90-1, 94-6, 105, 108-10,
114-6, 118-9, 121-2, 124,
126, 128-9, 133, 137, 142,
144, 146, 149, 150, 156,
161-2, 171, 179*
Stockton, Earl of, *166*
Strange, Curtis, *22, 57*
Sunesson, Fanny, *79*
Tarbuck, Jimmy, *166*
Taylor, J.H., *11*
Torrance, Bob, *93*
Torrance, Sam, *21, 25, 61,
63, 66, 70-7, 80, 84-5,
92-3, 105-6, 109, 113,
116, 118, 121, 124, 131-2,
135, 145, 150-1, 153, 161*
Townsend, Peter, *114*
Trevino, Lee, *17-8, 21, 24,
26*
Turnbull, Gordon, *140*
Tway, Bob, *51*
Vardon, Harry, *11*
Wadkins, Lanny, *20, 58, 89,
95-6, 105, 108, 111,
114-5, 118-9, 121, 124,
128, 131-2, 136-7, 139,
145-6, 150, 153*
Walser, Joe, *37*
Walton, Philip, *74*
Watson, Tom, *19, 20, 24,
26, 57, 61, 148, 155, 169*
Way, Paul, *26*
Weaver, Philip, *31, 150,
166*
Weetman, Harry, *15*
Weiskopf, Tom, *18, 88*
Whitcombe, Charles, *13*
Williams, Michael, *56*
Woosnam, Ian, *23, 51, 58,
61-3, 66, 68, 71, 85, 89,
92-3, 105-9, 112, 114-5,
118-9, 121-4, 126, 132,
136, 139, 142, 145, 150-2,
156, 161, 164, 167*
Wright, Ben, *135-6*

200